INTERNATIONAL PLAYTIME

CLASSROOM GAMES AND DANCES FROM AROUND THE WORLD

by Wayne E. Nelson and Henry "Buzz" Glass

Fearon Teacher Aids
Simon and Schuster Education Group

Editor: Carol Williams
Copyeditors: Lisa Schwimmer and Virginia Massey Bell
Cover Illustration and Design: Rose Sheifer
Illustration and Design: Rose Sheifer

ISBN 0-86653-990-5

Printed in the United States of America
1.9 8 7 6 5 4 3

ACKNOWLEDGMENTS

As with any undertaking of this magnitude, there are many people to thank, for without their encouragement, support, and help, this book would not have been possible. We give special thanks to:

- Ruth Nelson, who not only typed several drafts of the manuscript, but served as a sounding board and provided many helpful ideas and suggestions. Without her help, this book would never have been completed.

- Dr. Mel Aamodt and Lisa Davis for their map work.

- Our many friends, students, and professional colleagues who willingly contributed games and dances.

- Dr. Bob Anderson for his able assistance in translation and the correct pronunciation of Spanish words.

- Secretary Sally Pearce who gave unsparingly of her time and energy.

- Dr. William Morris, a colleague and friend, for being someone with whom we could talk.

- Our wonderful wives, Ruth and Frances, who gave us understanding and support during the long hours and involvement that this book required.

TABLE OF CONTENTS

INTRODUCTION

Think about your most memorable trips or vacations. What makes them so special? Maybe it is your memory of the beauty of the Grand Canyon, the remarkable temples of glittering gold in Thailand, or the colorful costumes and smiling faces at a Mexican fiesta. Experiencing the diversity around the world can create some of life's most treasured memories.

"International Playtime" is filled with a variety of games and dances from every continent to represent our worldwide cultural diversity. These games and dances, enjoyed by children from all over the world, have been collected from literature, friends, students, and professional colleagues.

The effect of doing a Caribbean dance or playing an Israeli game is to "walk a mile in another's shoes." Children can begin to understand and appreciate cultural differences. This wide presentation of world cultures can also be used as a springboard to other interdisciplinary projects on a selected culture or group.

Here then is an invitation for children to enjoy dance and movement in a multi-sensory program involving coordination, flexibility, strength, and balance. We hope that the use of these games and dances will help broaden your students' horizons, deepen their insights, and expand their feelings of affinity with students from different cultures around the world.

ABOUT THE AUTHORS

Wayne Nelson has taught Physical Education for 40 years. His experience includes 17 years of teaching in the public schools of Wisconsin and California at both the elementary and secondary levels and 23 years of teaching at the college level. He received his Bachelor's and Master's degrees in Physical Education from the University of Wisconsin, Madison, and his Doctorate from the University of New Mexico. Currently, Dr. Nelson is a professor in the Physical Education Department at California State University, Stanislaus, in Turlock, California. For the past 21 years, he has used extensive practical teaching experience to stimulate and motivate his students in Teacher Education at the under-graduate level and to conduct in-service workshops in the northern California area.

Henry "Buzz" Glass has been active in Physical Education and Movement Education for over 50 years. He was formerly the Supervisor of Elementary Physical Education for the Oakland Unified School District and a consultant in Special Education in Oakland, California. He now works as a National Consultant in Movement Education and presents workshops and seminars nationwide for teacher groups, school districts, colleges, and universities. "Buzz" has instructed multiple aspects of dance at preschool through university levels and has studied dance himself from many well-known dance teachers and cultural experts. "Buzz" received a Ford Foundation Fellowship to study dance in Mexico (1954-55) and was the founder and first president of the Folk Dance Federation of California. "Buzz" is the author of over twenty records and four books, the most recent being "The Rainy Day Survival Book," co-authored by Dr. Wayne Nelson.

ABOUT THE GAMES

This collection of games not only represents a variety of cultures, but is also geared to meet a variety of student needs, interests, and levels of ability. Select the games for your class according to their maturity level, past experience, and skill. Each game contains the following information to assist you.

GRADE LEVEL

A suggested grade level is indicated for each game. However, you will be the best judge of what games suit the maturity level and skill of your students. Also, many of the games can be adapted to achieve a more primary or advanced level.

SOMETHING ABOUT THE COUNTRY

Cultural information for each country is also included as information for the teacher and the students.

TYPE

Each game is classified as being either active or quiet and whether it is best played in a classroom or on the playground. Choose the games that best match your resources and the needs of your students.

EQUIPMENT

While some games require a few easy-to-find materials, others can be played with no additional resources or preparation. A list of equipment is provided so you can gather appropriate materials before the activity begins.

FORMATION

Included with the description of each game is a diagram showing the appropriate beginning formation. This symbol ◗ represents a student as he or she would appear if you were looking down from above. The dark part of each symbol represents the back of the students' heads. The lighter part indicates which way the child is facing.

DESCRIPTION

The abbreviation CW is used for clockwise and CCW is used for counterclockwise. Also, the directions "right" and "left" are always referred to as R and L. After you have read the description of a game and have a good understanding of how it is played, present the instructions clearly to your students. Here are some helpful suggestions to consider when presenting and playing the games.

- Have the attention of the entire class before beginning.

- Stand in front of the class when presenting directions.

- Project your voice so all can hear clearly.

- Explain the game briefly and precisely.

- Use descriptive picture words.

- Teach to the average student, but be patient with slow learners.

- Always have the equipment ready before the class begins.

- Place students in the correct beginning formation.

- Use the body as a directional guide.

- Have a signal for starting the game.

- Be enthusiastic and use a democratic approach.
- Use sound signals (whistles) sparingly.
- Overlook mistakes of participants.
- Be part of the class by participating whenever possible.
- Acquire a sensitivity to the interests of the class.
- Know when to stop the game.
- Have fun!

SAFETY

Safety should always be a prime consideration. In order to make the classroom safe for participation, prepare a plan in advance concerning which furniture should be moved and what hazards need to be eliminated. Teach students proper techniques of pushing and pulling to move desks and other classroom furniture. On the playground, be aware of potential hazards and take appropriate measures to minimize the risk to students' safety.

FORFEITS

Forfeits are used in many cultures as a penalty for an error or mistake in a game. This practice is thought to have originated in the custom of paying ransom for immunity from punishment for crimes. As used in games more recently, the main object of a forfeit is to add merriment through the ridiculous. Keep in mind that games should build self-esteem and confidence in your students, not tear it down. Make sure children do not feel defeated or belittled when they are deemed "out" or when required to pay a forfeit for a mistake.

The usual method of collecting forfeits is for each player, when he or she makes an error or mistake, to deposit with a designated person an object that identifys him or her. The object may be a ring, a pebble, a flower, a bit of ribbon, or an article of clothing. When the game is over, the forfeits are collected by a judge. A player, standing behind the judge, takes one object at a time from the pile of collected forfeits, holds it over the head of the judge so that the judge cannot see it and says,

"Heavy, heavy hangs over thy head. What must the owner do to redeem it?"

The judge then pronounces sentence. Part of the sport of redeeming forfeits is the ignorance of the judge as to who is the owner of the forfeit. For a list of ways to redeem forfeits see "Redeeming Forfeits" on page 223.

WHO'S IT? COUNTING OUT AND CHOOSING SIDES

In many games, it is necessary to appoint captains or leaders or to choose a player to be "IT." Counting-out rhymes and other methods of choosing players for games is one of the most interesting areas in the whole study of children's games. Counting-out rhymes probably originated in old superstitions and rites, including incantations of the old magicians and practices of divination by lot. These intricate formulas and rites are as fascinating as the games themselves. Methods of choosing sides are found all over the world. These ancient methods originated, like many children's games, from the serious practices of adults. For instance, classic literature has many references to casting lots, as in the "Iliad," when the heroes cast lots in Agamemnon's cap to decide who would go out to battle with Hector. Later, they chose by similar means their places in the funeral games for Patroclus. Here is an example of a counting-out rhyme.

"Onery, twoery, tickery tee,
Hallibone, crackabone, teneree,
Whackery, lackery, dackery, lore,
Hunkety, dunkety, twenty-four."

Other games require that players be divided into teams. Be sensitive to your students' feelings when forming teams. The traditional method of captains selecting players can leave the last children chosen feeling embarrassed and inferior. Counting off by twos is a quick way to form two equal teams. Or, divide players by birthdays—players whose birthdays are in the months of January through July form one team and those born in August through December form another. Or, ask students to clasp their own hands together. Players who have their right thumb on top form one team and players with their left thumb on top form another. If a game calls for several teams of equal size, a simple math problem can help out. Write a math problem on the chalkboard. Ask students to move into groups the size of the answer.

THE ROLE OF "IT"

A large proportion of all active games for children are IT games. Such games have a player who acts in opposition to the rest of the players. There can be either a high-power IT or a low-power IT. The high-power IT has a lot of power to control the movements of the other players. By proper use of this power, it is possible for IT to win or be successful with a minimum of skill. A game in which IT calls out a series of names, of which a particular name is the signal for the players to run to the opposite base, is an example of a high-power IT. IT has the power to place himself or herself close to the players before calling out the final name and is in a good position to tag someone.

The low-power IT has comparatively little power to control the movements of others, and therefore requires more skill to have a successful experience. A game in which no signal is given by IT, and the players run at will to the opposite base, is an example of a low-power IT. IT has no opportunity to chose the time, place, or opponent to tag. Winning and success depend in large measure upon the skill and cleverness of the player who is IT.

Be aware of the abilities of the children in a group to determine which kind of IT games are appropriate. There are students in every class who are highly skilled and who need the challenge of a low-power IT game. There are also students in every class who have moderate-to-low skills and need at least some high-power IT games to achieve success and to make the activity fun. A good mix of high- and low-power IT games will make such activities enjoyable and rewarding for all students.

ABOUT THE DANCES

In this collection, you will find rhythms that reflect both the traditional dance curriculum as well as today's society. While some dances promote enthusiasm and exuberance, others offer a feeling of peace and serenity. The variety of dance styles, steps, and rhythms offer the diversity necessary to meet the varied interests of your students.

Often teachers are uneasy with the challenge of teaching rhythmic activities. An extra effort has been made to include dances that will bring success to teachers with little or no experience teaching dance. This wide assortment of easy material will help promote a positive program with a more secure beginning. Each dance contains the following information to assist you in teaching the rhythms to your students.

GRADE LEVEL

A suggested grade level is indicated for each dance. However, many of the dances can be adapted on a more primary or advanced level by using the variations and suggestions at the end of each dance. A "+" indicates that the dance is suitable for recreational or adult use. Henry "Buzz" Glass, formerly a Supervisor of Special Education, has also included suggestions for adapting or simplifying dances to match the ability level of students with special needs.

BACKGROUND

The origin of each dance is provided so that you may take full advantage of choosing dances that complement a particular area of study. Background information can act as a springboard for launching into interdisciplinary activities based on a particular region. The dances from each country add insight into that country's customs and traditions.

MUSIC

A listing of suggested music is included for each dance, giving the name of the dance, the number, and the specific record or tape. The record or albums can be obtained by directly contacting the publisher or other distributers, such as your local teacher supply store. See page 228 for a listing of resources and addresses. The timing of the music (such as 2/4 or 3/4 time) is given so that you can substitute music that might be more readily available and still provide an appropriate rhythm for the dance steps.

FORMATION

Included with the description of each dance is a diagram showing the appropriate beginning formation. The wide variety of formations and pairing of partners or groups can help meet the needs and match the abilties of your students. No-partner dances eliminate pairing students in classes with uneven numbers of boys and girls. This type of dance relieves the anxiety some students feel about dancing with a partner or holding hands. No-partner dances are excellent levers to use with beginning groups to build rapport and security. Line dances, also known as "Kolo dances," facilitate a feeling of togetherness and harmony as dancers synchronize their rhythm and steps. Partner dances and mixers provide a frequent change of partners, keeping the interest level high. Circle dances, sitting dances, and dances in which students move about freely in a "scrambled egg" pattern all serve to meet a variety of interests.

DESCRIPTION

The counts column of the directions provides the number of counts necessary to execute the steps described on the right. A condensed description or title of each step has been set in bold type. This will allow you to quickly recall the steps at a glance once the dance has been learned. Or, before beginning the dance, you can quickly see what steps are required to perform the dance.

The abbreviation CW is used for clockwise and CCW is used for counterclockwise. Also, the directions "right" and "left" are always referred to as R and L.

For a list and description of common dance steps used in this collection, as well as the dance in which the steps appear, see "Forms of Dance and Movement" on page 225.

VARIATIONS AND SUGGESTIONS

This section includes helpful teaching hints, creative exploration and movement alternatives, and ways to adapt the dances to meet special needs and interests. For example, a dance intended for upper-elementary students can be adapted to incorporate fundamental patterns of locomotion and basic axial movements for primary groups. In the same way, suggestions are given that can make a relatively simple dance a challenge for the more mature and sophisticated dancer.

AFRICA
GAMES AND DANCES

Egypt

Sudan

Nigeria

Sierra Leone

Liberia

Ghana

Benin

Uganda

Congo

Kenya

Tanzania

South Africa

CHO-CHO-CHUCKIE

BENIN

TYPE
Active classroom game

SOMETHING ABOUT THE COUNTRY
The people of Benin eat very little meat and a lot of starch—yams being a large part of their diet. Palm oil from palm trees, a major crop in this agricultural country, is used for cooking as well as for smoothing on the skin. Kola nuts also grow here and are a symbol of friendship to the people of western Africa.

EQUIPMENT
✓ Large sponge

FORMATION

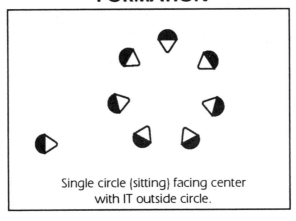

Single circle (sitting) facing center
with IT outside circle.

DESCRIPTION
IT carries a large sponge while running or skipping around the outside of the circle. Now and then, IT says "Cho-Cho-Chuckie" as though calling chickens. On one of the cluckings, IT drops the sponge behind a player. That player must stand, pick up the sponge, and chase IT around the circle. The player tries to tag IT before IT takes the player's place. If the player tags IT, then IT remains IT. If IT reaches the player's place safely, he or she stands on one foot while holding the other foot with one hand. The player becomes the new IT. (Players may change from one foot to the other as often as they like, but if IT sees a player not standing on one foot, he or she calls out the player's name, and that person becomes IT.) When all players are on one foot, except the last, IT shouts "It's raining!" Players at once raise an arm as though holding an umbrella and scatter in all directions with IT chasing them. The first player caught is IT for the next game.

OWARE
GHANA

TYPE
Quiet classroom game

SOMETHING ABOUT THE COUNTRY
Ghana has been referred to as the "country of festivals." Ghanaians celebrate feats of war, the beginning of the harvest, food, dance, and historical events. The highlights of the festivals center around music—dancing, singing, and drumming.

EQUIPMENT
None

FORMATION

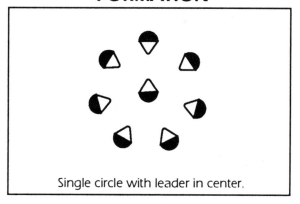

Single circle with leader in center.

DESCRIPTION
Players repeat whatever the leader says and imitate whatever the leader does. Then, the leader has all the players lie down. The leader counts to ten, at which point all players must immediately get up. The last player to get up is the new leader. (Ghanaians are usually shy and do not want to be imitated and therefore try hard not to be the last player to get up.)

TRAPPING TIGERS

NIGERIA

TYPE

Quiet classroom game

SOMETHING ABOUT THE COUNTRY

Nigerians have a rich oral tradition of storytelling, poetry, proverbs, and riddles. Dance and dramatic performance are rooted in traditional beliefs and are part of the everyday life of Nigerians.

EQUIPMENT

None

FORMATION

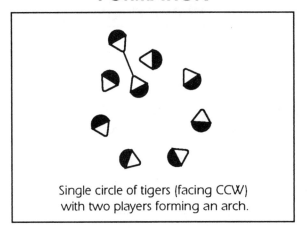

Single circle of tigers (facing CCW)
with two players forming an arch.

DESCRIPTION

Two players form an arch by holding their clasped hands above the other players' heads. The other players, known as the "tigers," sing the following song (to the tune of "Frere Jacques") as they march under the arch (the trap).

We are tigers. We are tigers.
We are brave. We are brave.
You will try to trap us.
You will try to trap us.
Catch us now! Spring the trap!

Players who are under the arch when the last word of the song is sung are caught and must form another arch. The game continues until all "tigers" are trapped. Remind players to march to the rhythm of the song and not to run.

BOTTLE RELAY

UGANDA

TYPE
Active playground game

SOMETHING ABOUT THE COUNTRY
Ugandan women often carry heavy items on their heads using a coiled-up cloth, called a kanga cloth, to cushion the load. Kanga cloth is purchased in ten-foot lengths and cut into two five-foot pieces—one piece of the cloth is for wearing and the other is used to cushion the load that is carried.

EQUIPMENT
✓ Small plastic bottles or cups

FORMATION

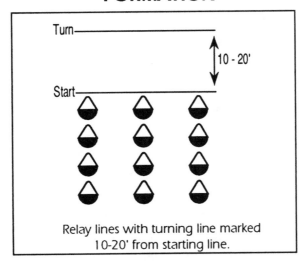

Relay lines with turning line marked
10-20' from starting line.

DESCRIPTION
Give each player a plastic bottle or cup to balance on his or her head. On a given signal, the first player on each team runs to the turning line while balancing the bottle on his or her head. The player touches the turning line, turns around, and runs back to tag the next player in line. After the runner has tagged the next player, he or she goes to the end of the line. If the bottle falls off the runner's head, the player must stop and replace it before moving forward. The team who finishes first wins.

ANIMAL KEEPERS

KENYA

TYPE
Active classroom game

SOMETHING ABOUT THE COUNTRY
Kenya has a rich wildlife that includes elephants, rhinoceros, cheetahs, and crocodiles. Many of these animals are on the endangered species list, and in order to protect these animals, Kenya has turned over six million acres of land into national parks and game reserves.

EQUIPMENT
✔ Pictures of wild animals

FORMATION

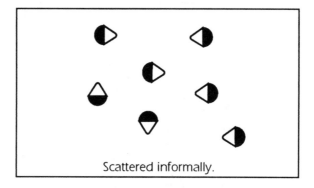

Scattered informally.

DESCRIPTION
Place a label with the name or picture of a wild animal on the back of each player without the player knowing what the animal is. Tell players that they are each taking an animal (named or pictured on their backs) to a safe location. Each player is the keeper of that animal and is to see that it arrives safely. Invite players to circulate and give hints to help each other discover the names of the animals on their backs. The hints should be accurate, but should also keep the players guessing as they move about and get to know one another. A player may give only one hint before moving on to the next person. Players can remove the labels from their backs and place them on their chests as soon as they guess the names of their animals.

DON-DON BA JI

SUDAN

TYPE
Active classroom or playground game

SOMETHING ABOUT THE COUNTRY

Although Sudan is basically an agricultural country, a small percentage of the people are nomads who move from place to place in search of grazing land for their cattle, sheep, camels, and goats. Sudanese nomads must raise several kinds of animals because some handle the lack of water and vegetation better than others. Livestock must also be protected from predators—such as the hyena.

EQUIPMENT
None

FORMATION

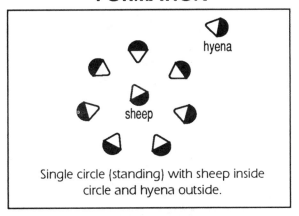

Single circle (standing) with sheep inside circle and hyena outside.

DESCRIPTION

Players clasp hands tightly and move CW while chanting:

> Don-don ba ji camelot.
> Don-don ba ji camelot.
> (Don-don ba ji means "hyena" and "sheep.")

The hyena attempts to crawl under or climb over the clasped hands, or break their grip in order to enter the circle. The players try to prevent the hyena from doing so. When the hyena gets inside the circle and captures the sheep, two other players become the hyena and the sheep.

HOP-SING GAME
LIBERIA

TYPE
Active classroom game

SOMETHING ABOUT THE COUNTRY
The majority of people in Liberia live in rural areas in farming villages. The schools are changing in Liberia, but many children still attend "bush schools" where they learn the customs, beliefs, and ceremonies of their people. Folktales, history, and legends are passed on to the children orally.

EQUIPMENT
✓ Music (African rhythm song)

FORMATION

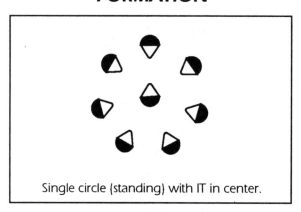

Single circle (standing) with IT in center.

DESCRIPTION
For this jumping game, players clap hands to the rhythm of an African song. (Any song with speed and action can be substituted. "Jingle Bells," without words, works well.) IT stands in the center of the circle with hands on hips, hopping from one foot to the other, always extending the leg that is in the air so that the toe points downward. IT advances to a child in the circle, hops, and extends the R or L foot with toe pointed. The player in the circle must respond quickly by hopping and pointing the same toe as the leader. For example, if both players extend their R leg with toe pointed, the toes will not hit each other. IT must then hop to another player in the circle and try again. If a player in the circle extends the wrong leg, the toes will hit. That player must then exchange places with IT.

CONGO

TYPE
Quiet classroom game

SOMETHING ABOUT THE COUNTRY
Nearly all the people living in the Congo are of Bantu origin. The Bantu use dance to express almost all the major events in life, including death. People join in with instruments, such as bells, horns, flutes, drums, or just their hands.

EQUIPMENT
None

FORMATION

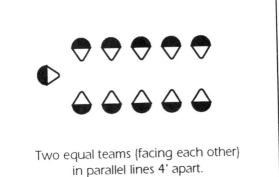

Two equal teams (facing each other)
in parallel lines 4' apart.

DESCRIPTION
In the Congo, boys and girls usually play this game separately. IT stands between the two lines and dances up and down the line while other players clap their hands rhythmically and chant "Ta Mbelle." Suddenly, IT stops before a player and extends a hand. The player must extend a hand at the same time. The object is for the player to match IT's choice of R or L hand. If the player does, he or she becomes IT. If not, the first IT goes on to another player.

HABA GABA
SIERRA LEONE

TYPE
Quiet classroom game

SOMETHING ABOUT THE COUNTRY .
Sierre Leone means "mountains of the lions." Some think the name comes from the notion that the sound of thunder echoing off the mountains sounds like the roar of a huge lion. Others say that Portuguese sailors saw the shapes of lions in the mountainous landscape—thus the name.

EQUIPMENT
✓ Beanbags
✓ Board or large piece of corrugated cardboard

FORMATION

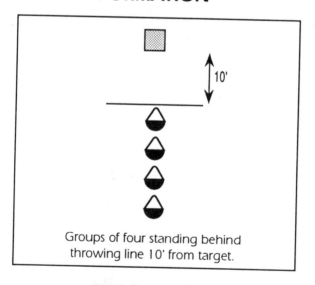

Groups of four standing behind
throwing line 10' from target.

DESCRIPTION
Cut three holes of different sizes (2, 3, and 4 inches in diameter) in the top, center, and bottom of the board or piece of cardboard. Number the holes with a 1, 2, or 3. Set the board at a 45-degree angle about ten feet from a marked throwing line. Players take turns pitching beanbags through the holes to score one, two, or three points. Players rotate being tossers, scorekeepers, or retrieving and throwing beanbags back to tossers. An inning consists of eight to ten tosses for each player. The player who scores the most points at the end of three innings is the winner.

TUG OF WAR

EGYPT

TYPE
Active playground game

SOMETHING ABOUT THE COUNTRY

This Egyptian tug of war game is depicted on the wall in the tomb of Mereruka on the outskirts of the ancient town of Memphis, the "city of the living," about twenty miles south of Cairo. Mereruka was a high official in the government of the Sixth Dynasty of this old kingdom. The game is played in Egyptian schools today representing continuity of sporting traditions and the influence of the ancient culture on modern practices.

EQUIPMENT
None

FORMATION

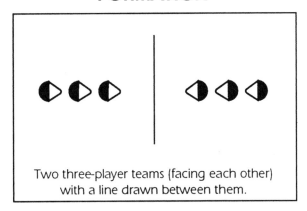

Two three-player teams (facing each other)
with a line drawn between them.

DESCRIPTION

The two front players, one from each team, are the leaders. The leaders clasp hands while the rest of the players hold on to the waist of the teammate in front of them. On a signal, each team tries to bring their opponents across the line to its side by pulling and leaning backwards. The spirit of competition is reflected in shouts by members of each team encouraging their leader, "Your arm is much stronger than his or hers!" While the others answer, "Our team is stronger than you are. Get hold of them, comrades!"

CHIKINCHA

TANZANIA

TYPE
Quiet classroom game

SOMETHING ABOUT THE COUNTRY
Tanzania is home to a nomadic tribe of native people called the Masai. The Masai are dependent on cattle for their livelihood, and the cow's milk is a major source of food. The milk is stored in gourds until solid and then mixed with cow's blood for a special Masai drink. The cow's dung is used as well. The Masai use the dung to build dome-shaped huts called "boma."

EQUIPMENT
None

FORMATION

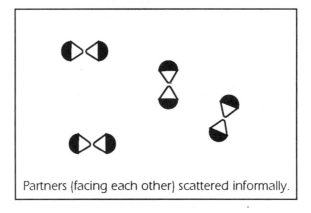

Partners (facing each other) scattered informally.

DESCRIPTION
Chikincha (chee-KEEN-cha) is a hand-clapping game for pairs, similar to Pease Porridge Hot. Chikincha is a nonsense word. The rest of the nonsense chant below translates as follows:

"I went to my uncle's and stayed two whole days. The third day I heard a knocking. A cow was mooing. Take off the rope."

Motions are performed to the words as described below:

ha	Players draw both hands lightly down the L arm of their partner.
chee▪KEEN▪cha	Partners clap, then smack the back of crossed hands together (L to partner's L and R to partner's R), and clap again.

chee▪KEEN▪cha	Repeat.
chee▪KEEN▪cha	Repeat.
(Repeat from the beginning.)	
NEE-lee▪KWEN-da	Players clap hands with partner and then clap own hands.
NEE-lee▪KWEN-da	Repeat.
KWAH-ma▪JOM-ba	Repeat.
KWAH-ma▪JOM-ba	Repeat.
NEE▪ka▪LA▪la	Players smack back of hands with partner four times.
SEE-koom▪BEE-lee	Players clap hands with partner and then clap own hands.
SEE-koom▪BEE-lee	Repeat.
NAH-ya▪TAH-too	Repeat.
NAH-ya▪TAH-too	Repeat.
NEE▪ka▪SEE▪kya	Players smack back of hands with partner four times.
N-gon▪GON-go	Players clap hands with partner and then clap own hands.
N-gon▪GON-go	Repeat.
NGOM-beh▪KAL-ya▪CHAL▪ya	Players smack back of hands with partner four times.
MKAH-tyeh-nee▪KAM-ba	Players clap hands with partner and then clap own hands.
MKAH-tyeh-nee▪KAM-ba	Repeat.
ha	Players draw both hands lightly down the Ŀ arm of their partner.
chee▪KEEN▪cha	Partners clap, then smack the back of crossed hands together (L to partner's L and R to partner's R), and clap again.
chee▪KEEN▪cha	Repeat.
chee▪KEEN▪cha	Repeat.

CLAPPING DANCE
GHANA

BACKGROUND
Dancers of all ages have performed and created interesting hand clapping games over the years. This hand clapping dance is based on a game from Ghana called "Tue Tue."

MUSIC (2/4)
"Panamanian Tambor," 1523, Folkraft.

FORMATION

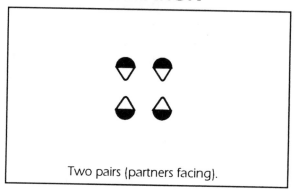

Two pairs (partners facing).

COUNTS	STEPS
8	**1. Clap Partner 2/Own 2** Clap both hands of partner (2 cts). Clap own hands (2 cts). Repeat (4 cts).
8	**2. Clap Neighbor 2/Own 2** Face the person beside you. Clap both hands of neighbor (2 cts). Clap own hands (2 cts). Repeat (4 cts).
16	**3. Clap Partner/Neighbor** Repeat Steps 1-2.
8	**4. Clap Partner's R and Own/Partner's L and Own** Clap R with partner and own hands (2 cts). Clap L with partner and own hands (2 cts). Repeat (4 cts).

8   **5. Clap Neighbor's R and Own/Neighbor's L and Own**
Face the person beside you.
Clap R with neighbor and own hands (2 cts).
Clap L with neighbor and own hands (2 cts).
Repeat (4 cts).

8   **6. Clap Partner's Palms/Clap Own**
With R palm down and L palm up, clap partner's hands (2 cts).
Clap own hands (2 cts).
Repeat (4 cts).

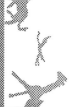

8   **7. Clap Neighbor's Palms/Clap Own**
Face the person beside you.
With R palm down and L palm up, clap neighbor's hands (2 cts).
Clap own hands (2 cts).
Repeat (4 cts).

16   **8. Slap Partner's Palms/Neighbor's Palms**
Repeat Steps 6-7.

VARIATIONS AND SUGGESTIONS

Creative Movements

Invite students to create their own clapping patterns.

Players can clap with the diagonal player. One couple may go low and the other high.

In between the clapping, players may add movement—such as jumping, kicking, hopping, stretching, hip-rocking, foot placing, or other dance patterns as a chorus (for the definitions of specific dance patterns, see page 225).

Mixer

Number dancers 1,2,3,4. While 1 and 3 do a basic pattern, 2 and 4 may move on to a new group.

West Indies Two-Step

For the definition of the two-step, see page 226.

When moving on to a new partner, step forward on L, step on ball of R beside L, step forward on L (2 cts).

Step forward on R, step on ball of L beside R, step forward on R (2 cts).
Cue the step by saying, "Flat-toe-flat, flat-toe-flat."

KYE KYE KULE
GHANA

BACKGROUND

Eager Ghanaian children delight in a variety of games involving songs and rhymes. Ghana's Kye Kye Kule (chay chay KOO-lay) is performed leader-group response style. Once the leader feels comfortable with the basic voice pattern, the variety of sensorimotor actions can be done as a singing game or chant. Encourage dancers to create their own actions as well.

MUSIC (4/4)

"Kye Kye Kule," Dance-a-Story Sing-a-Song, 110, Educational Activities.

FORMATION

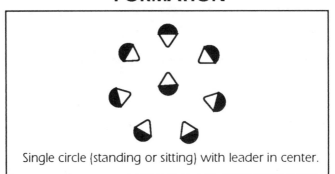

Single circle (standing or sitting) with leader in center.

Leader chants each phrase and group echos. Leader and group place hands on head, shoulders, waist, knees, and ankles as indicated by chant. (The leader and group say the last line in unison.)

WORDS	ACTIONS
Kye kye kule (chay chay KOO-lay)	Place hands on head.
Kye ko-finsa (chay KOE-fee-nsa)	Place hands on shoulders.
Kofi sa langa (koe-fee sa LAHN-ga)	Place hands on waist.
Ketekyi langa (kay-tay-chee LAHN-ga)	Place hands on knees.
Kum adende (koom a-DAYN-day)	Place hands on ankles.
Kum adende hey! (koom a-DAYN-day hay!)	Touch ankles and then jump upward, arms extended.

VARIATIONS AND SUGGESTIONS

English Version

Hands on your head now.	Place hands on head.
Hands on your shoulders.	Place hands on shoulders.
Hands on your hips now.	Place hands on hips.
Hands on your ankles.	Place hands on ankles.
Hands on your ankles, hey!	Touch ankles and then jump upward, arms extended.

Creative Movement

"Do a little hip swing" (swing hips side to side)
"Do a little side step" (extend foot sideways and back)
"Do a little looking" (look sideways L and R)
"Do a little rocking" (sitting, push off of floor with alternate hands)
End with "Do a little quiet" (said very quietly).

Invite children to form smaller groups and create their own leader-group response sequences.

"Do a little clapping"
"Do a little shaking"
"Do a little snapping"

Formation

Dancers can form a semicircle, lines facing forward, or sit in a cluster rather than a circle.

MOWRAH CAWKAH

NIGERIA

BACKGROUND

Though Nigeria is one of the wealthiest and most populated countries in Africa, there are not enough farmers to support the country, so much of Nigeria's food must be imported. Automobiles are scarce in Nigeria and there are no trains—buses, trucks, and taxis provide transportation throughout the country.

Mowrah Cawkah (MOW-rah KAW-kah) is a Nigerian action song learned from Joseph Oyewusi in 1970. Joseph Oyewusi came to this country as a result of meeting some American Peace Corps teachers who had traveled to his home country of Nigeria. Encourage dancers to sing along to the words that describe various methods of travel in Nigeria.

MUSIC (4/4)

"Mowrah Cawkah," Around the World in Dance 542, Educational Activities.

FORMATION

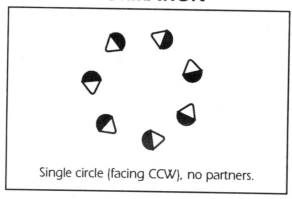

Single circle (facing CCW), no partners.

COUNTS	STEPS
	Introduction (wait in place)
16	**1. Chorus: Walking Steps** Moving CCW, take 32 walking steps around the circle, moving bent elbows in a natural, rhythmic opposition to feet. The steps are accented and on the flat of the foot. End facing center.
32	**2. Train Wheels (ch, ch, ch, ch)** Facing center, lean forward with bent elbows. Rotate arms forward in a small circle at the same time flexing knees.

32

3. Interlude: Walking Steps
Making a 1/4 turn to the R in place to face CCW, take
eight small walking steps.

8

4. Chorus: Walking Steps
Repeat Step 1.

32

5. Train Whistles (too, too, too)
With bent elbows, pull R arm downward as L extends
upward. Pull L arm downward as R extends upward.
Flex knees and keep a rhythmic bounce. Continue for the full
count.
Or, simply pull R bent elbow down-up, down-up continually.

32

6. Interlude: Walking Steps
Repeat Step 3.

8

7. Chorus: Walking Steps
Repeat Step 1.

32

8. Wagon Wheels, Lurching Wagons
Lean sideways to the L (2 cts) and then sideways to the
R (2 cts) while flexing knees, pantomiming lurching wagons
on country roads. Continue for the full count.

32

9. Interlude: Walking Steps
Repeat Step 3.

8

10. Chorus: Walking Steps
Repeat Step 1.

32

11. Paddling Canoes (Osumbo)
Pantomime paddling canoe on left side, right side,
while flexing knees. Continue for the full count.

32

12. Interlude: Walking Steps
Repeat Step 3.

8

13. Chorus: Walking Steps
Repeat Step 1.

32

14. Wheels and Drive Shaft (choopah, choopah, choopah, choopah, too, too)
Rotate bent elbows forward for 4 cts (choopah,
choopah, choopah, choopah).
Pull bent elbows backward-forward twice (too, too).
Continue for the full count.

VARIATIONS AND SUGGESTIONS

Formation

The dance could be done in a series of lines facing forward.

Step 1: Moving sideways to the L—step on L, close R, step on L, close R, and continue for 12 cts.

Stamp three times and hold (4 cts).

Repeat step-closes and stamps sideways R (for 16 cts).

Step 3: Facing forward, take eight walking steps.

Creative Movement

Invite students to create other ways of traveling in Nigeria, including rhythm patterns and sounds.

PATA PATA
SOUTH AFRICA

BACKGROUND

South Africa has two main tribes—Zulu and Xhosa. About 70% of the country is made up of black Africans. Cultural and artistic traditions are carried on through the generations and include a rich oral tradition of stories, poems, and folktales. Age-old dances, songs, and traditional dress still survive in rural areas.

Pata Pata is a dance that has spread worldwide because of its general appeal. This recreational dance is enjoyed by a great variety of groups and schools.

MUSIC (4/4)
"Pata Pata," 0732, Reprise (see Ed Kremers' Folk Showplace).

FORMATION

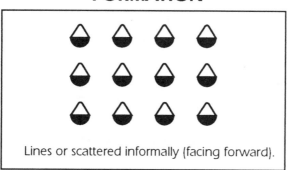

Lines or scattered informally (facing forward).

COUNTS	STEPS
16	Introduction (wait in place)

4

1. Single Extend
For a definition of a single extend, see page 227.
Extend R foot sideways R and step on R beside L (2 cts).
Extend L foot sideways L and step on L beside R (2 cts).

4

2. Toes-Heels, Heels-Toes
With weight on heels, turn toes outward and then
   with weight on toes, swivel heels outward (2 cts).
Reverse the action bringing heels together and toes
   together (2 cts).

4

3. Step-Lift
Lift bent R leg up and over L leg and then touch R toe
   beside L (2 cts).
Lift bent R leg up and over L leg and step on R beside
   L (2 cts).

4. Kick-Turn

Turn 1/4 R by kicking L foot forward and pivoting on R.
Moving backward, step LRL. (Each time the dance
repeats, dancers face a new wall.)

VARIATIONS AND SUGGESTIONS

Creative Movement

Invite students to create hand and body motions with the step-lift, kick-turn.

Primary

Step 1: Same
Step 2: Jump with feet apart and hold (2 cts).
   Jump with feet together and hold (2 cts).
Step 3: Same
Step 4: Do not pivot R on the kick-turn. Dancers remain facing forward.

Advanced

Step 1: Do a double extend to the R, extending R to side, bringing R
   beside L, extending R to side, bringing R beside L (4 cts). For the
   definition of a double extend, see page 227.
   Repeat double extend to the L (4 cts).
   Repeat both sides (8 cts).
Step 2: Do toes-heels and heels-toes twice (8 cts).
Step 3: Same
Step 4: Add clap when foot is kicked out to make 1/4 turn R then step
   backward LRL.

ASIA
GAMES AND DANCES

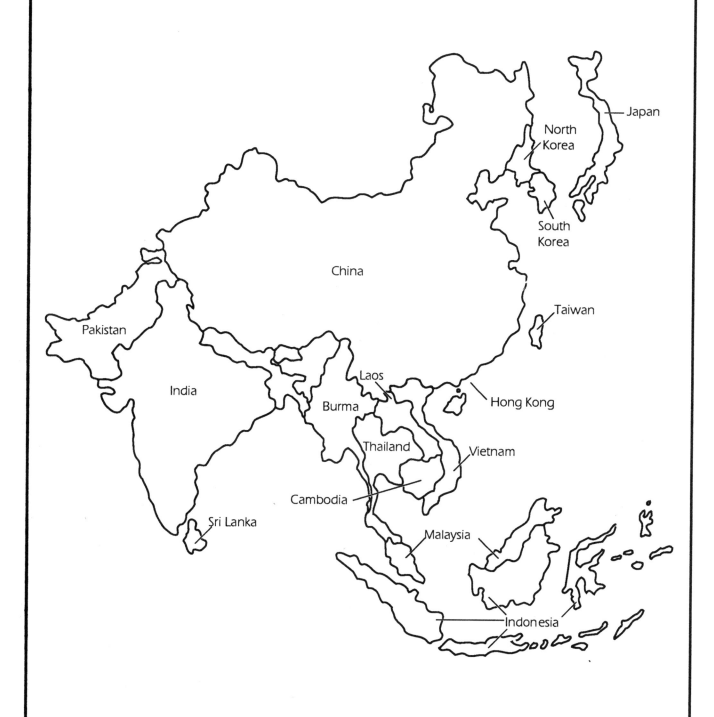

CLAPSTICK BLIND MAN'S BLUFF

TAIWAN

TYPE
Active playground game

SOMETHING ABOUT THE COUNTRY
Most children in Taiwan speak Mandarin, the Chinese national language. But some also speak another Chinese dialect at home, as well as English at school. Most TV programs in Taiwan have subtitles in Chinese, so young students are able to learn Chinese characters as they listen and watch TV.

EQUIPMENT
✓ Two sticks (plastic tubes) per player
✓ Blindfold
✓ Handkerchief

FORMATION

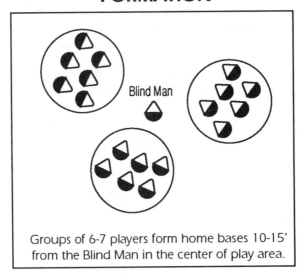

Blind Man

Groups of 6-7 players form home bases 10-15' from the Blind Man in the center of play area.

DESCRIPTION
Each player, except the Blind Man, has two sticks that make a loud noise when clapped together. Before being blindfolded, the Blind Man should make sure he or she knows the location of the "homes." The Blind Man is blindfolded and given a handkerchief with which to tag players. Two players must always be in motion, running to exchange places and clapping their sticks as they run. Players signal those with whom they want to exchange spots (before they run) to avoid collision and confusion. The player tagged by the Blind Man's handkerchief becomes the next Blind Man.

SATHI KHOJ (LOST A COUPLE)

PAKISTAN

TYPE
Active classroom or playground game

SOMETHING ABOUT THE COUNTRY
Pakistani children enjoy many of the same activities the children in the United States and other countries enjoy. These include team sports, such as cricket, soccer, and volleyball, as well as playing hopscotch, marbles, and flying kites.

EQUIPMENT
None

FORMATION

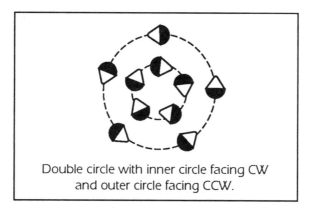

Double circle with inner circle facing CW and outer circle facing CCW.

DESCRIPTION
To make a double circle, have players first stand in a single circle. Number players off by twos. The "twos" take a step forward and form a smaller circle. Each pair of players consists of a "one" and a "two." The inner circle turns L and the outer circle turns R. The partners in each pair will be facing opposite directions. On a given signal, both circles begin to walk fast in opposite directions. On the signal to stop, players find their partners (players who were standing side by side at the beginning). Partners hold hands and sit down wherever they can. The last pair to sit down is out. The game continues until there is only one pair remaining.

O-O-OH-SOOM

THAILAND

TYPE
Quiet classroom game

SOMETHING ABOUT THE COUNTRY

Thai adults and children alike know that the key to their country's future lies in education. Literacy is on the rise in Thailand. When young people aren't sharpening their academic skills, some Thai children enjoy the popular pastime of kite fighting.

EQUIPMENT
None

FORMATION

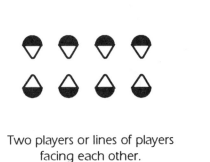

Two players or lines of players
facing each other.

DESCRIPTION

Players put their R hand on one ear and say "O-O-Oh-Soom!" On the word "Soom," players bring down their R hands and make one of three hand signs:

flat hand (paper)
fist (rock)
two extended fingers (scissors)

Partners facing each other determine which player wins according to the consequence of each hand sign:

Paper wraps the rock (paper wins).
Rock breaks the scissors (rock wins).
Scissors cut the paper (scissors win).

The winning player scores a point and the game begins again. The player with the most points after ten games is the winner.

CHUNG TOU TEH TOU (PLANT BEANS, REAP BEANS)

HONG KONG

TYPE
Active classroom or playground game

SOMETHING ABOUT THE COUNTRY
Hong Kong has a growing season that lasts all year long. Traditionally, Hong Kong women tend tiny farms by hand, while the men work in local industry. As soon as the children are old enough, they are expected to work as well.

EQUIPMENT
✓ Ten tokens (checkers, stones, marbles, or beans)
✓ Ten paper plates

FORMATION

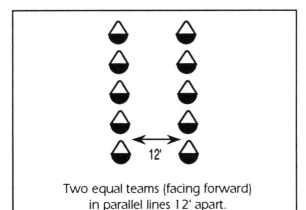

12'

Two equal teams (facing forward)
in parallel lines 12' apart.

DESCRIPTION
Place five plates in front of each team about five feet from the first player. Give the first player on each team five tokens representing beans to be planted. The leader gives the signal for the game to start and the first player in each line runs to the plates and places a token in the center of each, as if planting beans. The player then runs to the end of the line, touching the outstretched hand of the second player at the head of the line as he or she passes. The second player runs to the plates and gathers up the tokens one at a time as if reaping the beans. This player then runs to the end of the line giving the tokens to the third player in line as he or she passes. The third player runs to the plates and places a token in the center of each. The planting and reaping continues until all players have had a turn. The team that finishes first is the winner.

STATIONS

SRI LANKA

TYPE
Active classroom or playground game

SOMETHING ABOUT THE COUNTRY
In Sri Lanka, a bicycle is used for much more than recreation. Like China, Sri Lanka's main form of transportation is the bicycle. Sri Lankans use the bicycle to transport goods to and from market instead of walking long distances. It is no wonder the bicycle is often a family's most prized possession.

EQUIPMENT
✓ Marker
✓ Masking tape

FORMATION

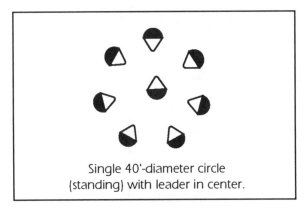

Single 40'-diameter circle
(standing) with leader in center.

DESCRIPTION
Give each player the name of a railway station, city, or other geographical entity in Sri Lanka (for example, cities like Kandy, Galle, Badulla, Yala, Maho, and so on). Use masking tape and a marker to mark the names of the stations on the floor in a circle. The player, standing in the center of the circle, is given the name "Fort Station" (the central station in Colombo, the capital city in Sri Lanka). The center player says (for example) "Train runs from Colombo to Kandy." The two players standing on these stations change places, while the center player tries to take one of the vacant stations before it can be filled. The player unable to take a vacant station becomes the center player. If the center player says "Trains run express," all players change stations and the center player tries to take one of the places. The center player can call out the names of up to three stations at once.

ZHAO LINGXIU (FIND THE LEADER)

CHINA

TYPE
Quiet classroom game

SOMETHING ABOUT THE COUNTRY
Many cities in China have "children's palaces"—places where children go after school to study certain skills, develop hobbies, and pursue special interests. Teachers organize activities there that are fun for the children—but also educational.

EQUIPMENT
None

FORMATION

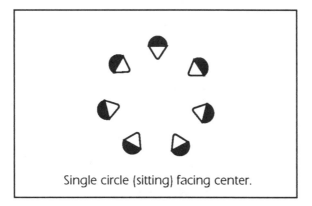

Single circle (sitting) facing center.

DESCRIPTION
One player leaves the room. The other players choose a leader. The leader begins an action, such as clapping or snapping his or her fingers. Other players copy the leader's actions. The leader should change the action frequently. When the player outside the classroom is asked to come in, he or she has three guesses to name the leader. If he or she guesses correctly, the leader leaves the room, while another player is chosen to be the new leader. If the player is unable to guess the leader's identity, that player must do a stunt that the other players tell him or her to do, such as hopping around the room on one foot or walking around the room and greeting each classmate with a smile. Encourage students to think of creative stunts, such as asking a player to laugh in one corner of the room, sing in the second corner, dance in the third corner, and whistle in the last corner.

ANG-KONNH

CAMBODIA

TYPE
Quiet classroom game

SOMETHING ABOUT THE COUNTRY
In early spring, Cambodians say good-bye to winter with a·celebration that includes the first planting of the year. During the celebration, musicians play carved instruments while a man leads a pair of oxen pulling a plow. As the man plows, a woman follows, sprinkling seeds into the furrow.

EQUIPMENT
✓ Stones, peach pits, or walnuts

FORMATION

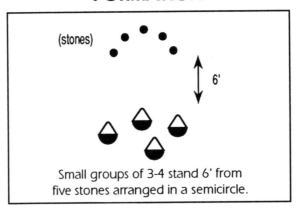

(stones)

6'

Small groups of 3-4 stand 6' from five stones arranged in a semicircle.

DESCRIPTION
This game is often played on New Year's Day using fruitstones. Players in turn try to hit each stone in the formation by throwing stones of their own. The first stone is thrown with the R hand and the second stone with the L. The third stone is thrown underneath the R knee. The fourth stone is thrown under the L knee. The last throw is a backward throw either with the R hand over the L shoulder or the L hand over the R shoulder. When a player misses, the next player takes a turn. On a second turn, a player starts throwing at the point where he or she left off on the last turn. The first player to get through all the motions correctly wins.

CHOPSTICKS JACK

LAOS

TYPE
Quiet classroom game

SOMETHING ABOUT THE COUNTRY
The majority of Laotians are farmers and one of the main crops in Laos is rice. In the highlands, corn, cotton, and tobacco are raised as well. The houses in the highlands of Laos are built 6 to 8 feet above the ground on wooden posts.

EQUIPMENT
✓ Ten chopsticks
✓ One small ball or round nut per player or group

FORMATION

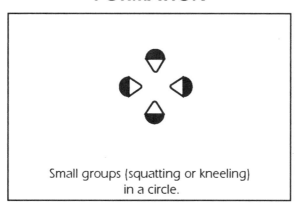

Small groups (squatting or kneeling)
in a circle.

DESCRIPTION
The first player tosses the chopsticks on the floor. The player then tosses the ball into the air, quickly picks up a stick with the same hand, and catches the ball before it bounces. The player continues to pick up the sticks, one at a time, until he or she fails to pick up a stick or is unable to catch the ball before it bounces. When a miss occurs, the next player tosses the sticks on the floor and picks up the sticks one at a time before catching the tossed ball. The winner is the player who picks up the most sticks in one turn.

INDIA

TYPE
Active playground game

SOMETHING ABOUT THE COUNTRY
Just like children in the United States, Indian children enjoy getting together and playing games during lunch breaks and after school. For this game of kabbaddi, children use their wits to be clever and quick—and must be good at holding their breath as well!

EQUIPMENT
None

FORMATION

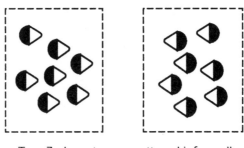

Two 7-player teams scattered informally within boundaries.

DESCRIPTION
One player from Team 1 crosses the boundary and steps in the area of Team 2. The player attempts to tag players from Team 2. The player from Team 1 must tag the Team 2 players while holding his or her breath. To ensure that the player is holding his or her breath, the player must chant the word "kabbaddi" constantly. Tagged players are deemed "out" only if the player returns to his or her area without taking a breath (touching the boundary line is considered a return). If a player loses his breath, he or she is considered out. The game continues as a player from Team 2 steps into the boundary area of Team 1 and tries to tag players. The team with remaining players when the opposing team players are all deemed "out" is the winner.

MEMUTAR PINGGAN (PLATE SPINNING)

MALAYSIA

TYPE
Quiet classroom game

SOMETHING ABOUT THE COUNTRY
The wonderful art form of batik comes from Malaysia. Beautifully designed fabrics are created by covering parts of cloth with wax and then dyeing the cloth. The areas covered with wax resist the dye.

EQUIPMENT
✓ Frisbee (plate)

FORMATION

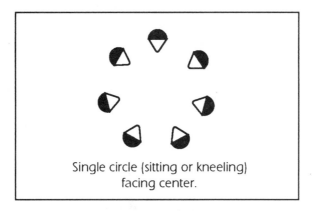

Single circle (sitting or kneeling)
facing center.

DESCRIPTION
One player spins the Frisbee or plate on its edge in the center of the circle and calls out one of the other player's names. The player whose name is called attempts to catch the plate before it falls. He or she then spins the plate again and calls out the name of another player. A player can stop the plate completely and then respin it, or respin the plate without bringing it to a stop. If a player is not able to catch the plate before it stops spinning, a point is scored against him or her. At the end of a set period of time, the players who scored points must pay a forfeit (see page 9).

PUTUNG PUTUNG

KOREA

TYPE
Quiet classroom game

SOMETHING ABOUT THE COUNTRY
Because Korea was such a poor country for so long, people learned to entertain themselves using few or no materials. Evenings are spent with family, and the children play popular games, such as "putung putung," "kawi bawi bo (paper, scissors, rock)," and "blind man's bluff."

EQUIPMENT
None

FORMATION

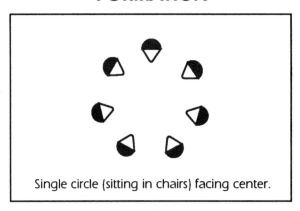

Single circle (sitting in chairs) facing center.

DESCRIPTION
"Putung" (pooh-toong) is a Chinese word describing the sound of a frog hitting the water and is similar in meaning to the English word "plop." Choose one player to be the leader. The leader starts the game by saying "one frog." The second player to his or her R says "two eyes." The third player says "four legs" and the fourth player says "putung." The fifth player says "jump in the water." The sixth player starts the series over from the beginning, but says "two frogs." The game continues with "four eyes," "eight legs," and "putung, putung," but only one call of "jump in the water." The game continues with the addition of another frog on the completion of each series. When a player says the wrong number or order, he or she is out of the game. The game can also be played with all players remaining in the game, even if a mistake is made. Determine a length of time the game will be played. Points can be scored against players who make a mistake. At the end of the game the player with the fewest points is the winner.

WORA-WORA TJINTJIN (RING AND LOOSE STRING GAME)

INDONESIA

TYPE
Quiet classroom game

SOMETHING ABOUT THE COUNTRY
Indonesia is a nation of 13,677 islands spanning over 3,000 miles. This fascinating area boasts twenty-five languages and two hundred and fifty dialects.

EQUIPMENT
✓ Thin, durable string
✓ Ring or small washer

FORMATION

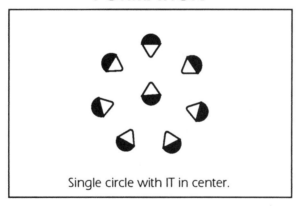

Single circle with IT in center.

DESCRIPTION
Put the ring on a piece of string that is a bit longer than the circumference of the circle of players. Tie the ends of the string together in a very small knot (ring must be able to pass over knot). Each player holds the string with both hands. Players move their hands while IT tries to guess where the ring is. The position of the ring is known to all in the beginning. The player with the ring must pass the ring to another person without IT finding out where the ring is. Players all shout together "Wora-Wora Tjintjin" (War-ra war-ra chin-chin) as they pass the ring faster and faster. IT shouts "stop" anytime after players have shouted the game's name at least four times. IT then gets one chance to guess where the ring is. If IT guesses correctly, the person caught with the ring becomes IT. In Indonesia, if IT guesses incorrectly, he or she must give the player who was misjudged a piggy-back ride around the circle and must be IT again. For safety reasons, choose an alternate consequence for incorrect guesses.

FUROSHIKI MAWASKI (SCARF PASSING GAME)

JAPAN

TYPE
Active classroom game

SOMETHING ABOUT THE COUNTRY
In the Japanese culture, people take great care in wrapping gifts. A beautifully wrapped gift is a sign of respect. A furoshiki is a special cloth used for wrapping gifts that can later be used for carrying objects, such as books or a lunch.

EQUIPMENT
✔ Scarves (one for every 3-4 players)
✔ Music (with a fast tempo)

FORMATION

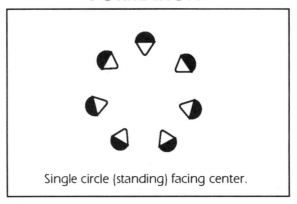

Single circle (standing) facing center.

DESCRIPTION
The game begins when the music starts. Players holding a furoshiki tie it around their necks, nod their heads twice, and then untie the furoshiki and pass it on to the player on the R. Players try to avoid having two furoshikis at one time while trying to make another player get caught with two. When a player receives two furoshikis at once, he or she is out of the game. The winners are the last two players left in the game.

In another version of the game, the last two players stand facing each other and place the palms of their hands together. Standing with their feet together, each pushes against the other's palms to make the other player lose his or her balance and step backward. The player who steps backward first loses the competition.

KICK-SWING

VIETNAM

TYPE
Active classroom game

SOMETHING ABOUT THE COUNTRY
Under showers of fireworks, the Vietnamese celebrate Tet—the Vietnamese New Year—for three days. This is a special occasion when traditional customs are observed and homage is paid to one's ancestors. It is a time to look back on the past, enjoy the present, and look forward to the future.

EQUIPMENT
✓ Small coin
✓ Tissue paper
✓ Wrapping paper
✓ String

FORMATION

Two equal teams (facing each other)
in parallel lines 4-10' apart.

DESCRIPTION
Wrap a small coin in wadded tissue paper. Tie up the tiny package in wrapping paper as though it were a little bag. Shred the top of the "bag" and spread out the little fringes. Players kick the bag back and forth from team to team with the bottoms of their feet. The object is to keep the package in the air. The team that touches the package with their hands or lets it drop scores a point against themselves. Choose a number of points (such as ten) at which one team loses the game.

MYAN, MYAN (I PASS THE SHOE FROM ME TO YOU)

BURMA

TYPE
Quiet classroom game

SOMETHING ABOUT THE COUNTRY
The favorite sports of Burma are soccer and kick boxing. Both of these sports enjoy a growing popularity in the United States. Soccer and kick boxing are spectator sports—but try your hand at a popular game using every part of your body except your hands to keep a small ball up in the air!

EQUIPMENT
✔ Small wooden block or eraser for each player

FORMATION

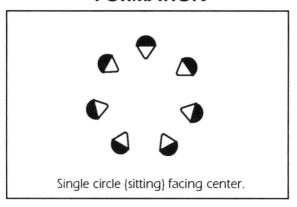

Single circle (sitting) facing center.

DESCRIPTION
Each player holds a wooden block or eraser. Players pass the wooden blocks as they chant the following:

"You must pass this shoe from me to you.
You must pass this shoe and do just like I do."

On the word "pass" in the second line, the "shoe" is passed to the R (but not released). On the word "and," players move the "shoe" back in front of them. On the words "do just like I do," players move their hand R, L, R leaving the "shoe" with the player on their R.
Burmese children use this chant:

"Myan Myan pay jah bah oh mahsway ah poun doh,
Myan myan pay jah bah ma pay nine yin pyin twet."

TANKO BUSHI
JAPAN

BACKGROUND

Tanko Bushi (TAHN-ko BOO-shee) is probably the best known Japanese folk dance. Translated as the "coal miner's dance," it depicts different stages of mining coal through pantomimic action.

MUSIC (4/4)

"Tanko Bushi," MH 2010, Folk Dancer (see Ed Kremers' Folk Showplace).

FORMATION

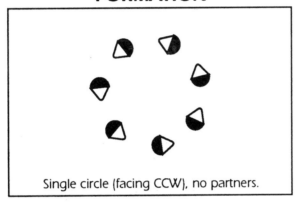

Single circle (facing CCW), no partners.

COUNTS	STEPS
16	Introduction (wait in place)

1. Dig the Coal
8

Pretend to hold a shovel with both hands. Facing slightly R, lift shovel and raise pointed R toe by L knee. Thrust shovel downward while touching R toe to floor (2 cts).
Repeat (2 cts).
Face slightly L and repeat action, digging with L (4 cts).

2. Throw the Coal
4

Touch R toe forward, at the same time throwing coal with pretend shovel backward over R shoulder and then lower R heel (2 cts).
Touch L toe forward, throwing coal over L shoulder and then lower L heel (2 cts).

4   ### 3. Look Through Coal Dust
Step backward on R, turning slightly R, at the same time
placing L hand above eye, as if shading, as R hand and
arm extend backward (2 cts).
Step backward on L, turning slightly L, shading with R
hand and allowing L arm to extend backward (2 cts).

8   ### 4. Push the Coal Cart
Step forward on R as both hands push pretend cart (2 cts).
Step forward on L as both hands push cart (2 cts).
Step forward on bent R knee while bringing both hands
down and out to side (1 ct).
Step back on L in place straightening (1 ct).
Clap hands at chest level and hold (2 cts).

4   ### 5. Clap
Clap three times and hold.

Ending
Repeat entire dance (Steps 1-5).
Clap slowly five times.
Repeat dance twice.
Clap slowly five times.
(The five slow claps occur after each two repetitions of the
dance.)

VARIATIONS AND SUGGESTIONS

Sitting Dance

Step 1: Same

Step 2: Same

Step 3: Place L hand to forehead and extend R backward. Place R
hand to forehead and extend L backward.

Step 4: Push hands at chest level forward and backward two times (4 cts).
Fan hands down and backward (1 ct) and retrace (1 ct).
Clap hands at chest level three times and hold (4 cts).

CHINESE FRIENDSHIP DANCE
CHINA

BACKGROUND

Chinese music sounds very different from Western music. Some traditional Chinese instruments include a "gin," which is a seven-stringed instrument; a mouth organ made of seven bamboo pipes called a "sheng;" and a lute-like instrument called a "pipa." There are also two types of traditional flutes—one is called a "xiao" and the other a "di." This version of the Chinese Friendship Dance has been especially arranged for elementary students by Henry "Buzz" Glass. The music was recorded in China.

MUSIC (4/4)

"Chinese Friendship Dance," Dances Around the World 572, Educational Activities.

FORMATION

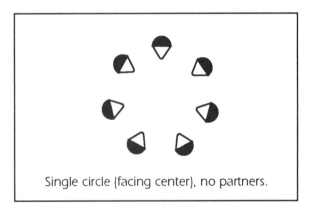

Single circle (facing center), no partners.

COUNTS	STEPS
8	Introduction (wait in place)

Part I

COUNTS	STEPS
8	**1. Clap Hands and Tilt Head** Clap hands by L shoulder, tilting head L and hold (2 cts). Clap hands by R shoulder, tilting head R and hold (2 cts). Repeat (4 cts).
8	**2. Walk Forward/Backward** Moving toward center with hands joined, walk forward LRLR (4 cts). Moving away from center, walk backward LRLR (4 cts).
8	**3. Clap Hands and Tilt Head** Repeat Step 1.

4. Extend L/R and Stamp
6

Point L toe forward and return to R (2 cts).
Point R toe forward and return to L (2 cts).
Stamp L by R and hold (2 cts).

5. Bow and Up/Wave Hands
16

Bow from the waist (2 cts) and straighten (2 cts).
Repeat (4 cts).
Extend hands over head and wave (8 cts).

Part II

6. Clap Hands and Tilt Head
8

Repeat Step 1.

7. Walk Forward/Backward
8

Repeat Step 2.

8. Skip/Step-Closes/Stamp
16

Moving CW with hands joined, take eight skips
beginning on L (8 cts).
Step sideways on L, close R to L, step sideways on L,
close R to L, step sideways on L, and close R to L (6 cts).
Stamp L beside R and hold (2 cts).

9. Wave Hands
8

Extend hands overhead and wave (8 cts).
Repeat entire dance (Part I and Part II).

VARIATIONS AND SUGGESTIONS

Dancers may skip freely at random for Step 8 rather than CW, but still end facing center for the three step-closes and stamp. End waving hands over head.

CARIBBEAN
GAMES AND DANCES

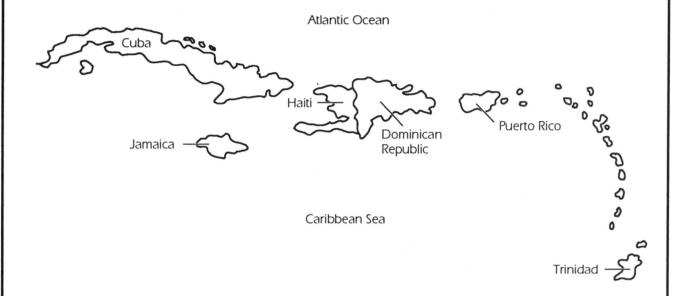

Atlantic Ocean

Cuba

Haiti

Dominican
Republic

Puerto Rico

Jamaica

Caribbean Sea

Trinidad

All of these islands (including those not labeled) are in the West Indies.

SALLY WATER

JAMAICA

TYPE
Quiet classroom game

SOMETHING ABOUT THE COUNTRY
Jamaica, well-known for its Reggae music, is a tropical island with warm sandy beaches, rocky mountains, lowlands, and coastal plains. Beautiful flowering plants, such as hibiscus, orchids, and poinsettias, grow wild on this lush island.

EQUIPMENT
None

FORMATION

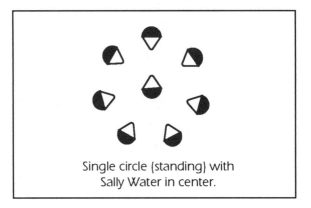

Single circle (standing) with
Sally Water in center.

DESCRIPTION
Players standing in the circle join hands. Sally Water crouches in the center of the circle. As players say "Rise, Sally, Rise," Sally Water slowly stands up. Sally Water brushes away imaginary tears, turns first one way and then the other, and chooses a partner from the circle. Sally Water and his or her partner hold hands and twirl together in a rapid turning dance. Then the partner chosen becomes the new Sally Water. Jamaican music may be used to add more enjoyment to the game.

COUNTING OUT GAME

TRINIDAD

TYPE

Quiet classroom game

SOMETHING ABOUT THE COUNTRY

"Carnival" is a huge festival in Trinidad celebrated two days before Ash Wednesday. This is such a major event in Trinidad that it is in the planning stages all year long. There are wonderful parades with dancing, Calypso, brilliantly colored costumes, and steel drums. The steel drums are made from discarded oil drums. The tops of the oil drums are hammered in such a way as to make specific sounds when drumming.

EQUIPMENT

None

FORMATION

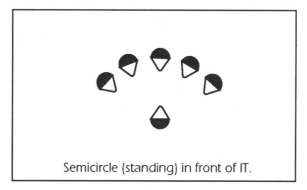

Semicircle (standing) in front of IT.

DESCRIPTION

IT stands with a hand held out, palm down, about shoulder high. Other players hold their pointer fingers under IT's hand, touching his or her palm. IT says:

"Ziggeddy, ziggeddy,
Marble stone,
Pointer, pointer, bouff!
Kisskillindy, kisskillindy,
Pa. . . pa. . . poriff!"

On the last word, IT grabs at the touching fingers, which are hastily pulled away. The player whose finger is caught becomes the next IT. Caution IT to be careful not to hurt anyone when grabbing at the fingers.

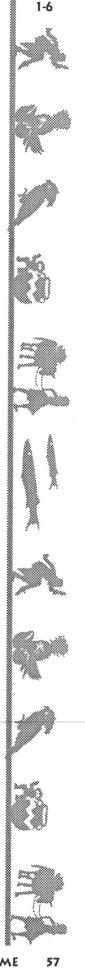

AINSI FONT, FONT, FONT DES ZAMI DE PAPA LA CHAISE (THUS DO, DO, DO THE FRIENDS OF PAPA LA CHAISE)

HAITI

TYPE

Active classroom game

SOMETHING ABOUT THE COUNTRY

Haiti is a small Caribbean island close to Cuba. Haitian farmers raise coffee and cacao. Cacao is used to make cocoa and chocolate. Some farmers raise their crops on slopes so steep that they have to anchor themselves with rope so they don't slide down the hillside. Most Haitians speak Creole, a french-based language.

EQUIPMENT

None

FORMATION

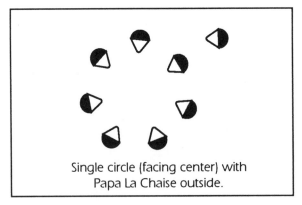

Single circle (facing center) with
Papa La Chaise outside.

DESCRIPTION

Papa La Chaise walks quickly CW around the outside of the circle of "des zami" (friends). When it is least expected, he or she touches a player. This player leaves his or her place and walks quickly CCW while Papa La Chaise continues walking CW. When the two players meet, they bow, shake hands, spin around, and shake hands again. Then the rest of the players

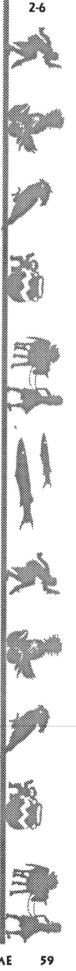

standing in the circle address the following verse to Papa La Chaise (or Momzelle La Chaise):

Bonsoir, bonsoir (Good evening, good evening),
Papa La Chaise
Comment ou yé? (How are you?)
Quand m'a-lé ca ma dit la caille (When I go home shall I say)
Comment ou yé? (How are you?)

After the friends have spoken the words, both players run for the empty place in the circle. The player who is left without a place becomes the next Papa La Chaise or Momzelle La Chaise.

CUBA AND SPAIN

CUBA

TYPE

Active playground game

SOMETHING ABOUT THE COUNTRY

Cuba gained its independence from Spain in 1898, but the Spanish influence in Cuba is very apparent in their architecture, museums, and statues. Havana, Cuba's capital, has three Spanish castles—the Castle of the Moors, the Castle of the Point, and the Castle of the Force.

EQUIPMENT

None

FORMATION

Two equal teams (facing each other)
in parallel lines 10' apart.

DESCRIPTION

One team is Spain and the other team is Cuba. A player from Spain is chosen to go to Cuba. All the Cuban players hold out their hands, palms up. The Spanish player rubs his or her R hand over the palms of each player in the Cuban line. Finally, the Spanish player claps the palm of a Cuban player signaling the Cuban player to chase him or her to Spain's side. If the Cuban player catches the other player before reaching the Spanish side, the Cuban player takes the Spanish player to Cuba's side. If the Cuban player doesn't catch the Spanish player, the Cuban player goes back to his or her original place in line. The game continues with a player from Cuba visiting Spain. The object is to get all of the players on one side. If this is not accomplished by the end of the play period, the side with the largest number of players is declared the winner.

THE STONES

PUERTO RICO

TYPE

Quiet classroom game

SOMETHING ABOUT THE COUNTRY

Puerto Rico has a diverse population. Many people of different nationalities have settled and married in this country. Besides the native Puerto Ricans, called "Taínos" or "Arawaks," Africans, Spaniards, Chinese, Italians, Lebanese, Venezuelans, and "continentales" (people from the United States) have made their home in Puerto Rico.

EQUIPMENT

✓Stones (2 large and 2 small)
✓Masking tape

FORMATION

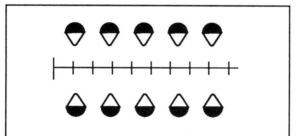

Two equal teams (facing each other) in parallel lines 3-6' apart with a line marked down the center of the two teams. The line has measurement marks indicating feet.

DESCRIPTION

Designate a captain for each team and give each team a large stone. Team captains place the large stones side by side at the front of a line marked an equal distance from the opposing sides. Each captain holds one of the small stones. Players hold their hands behind their backs and the captain of Team 1 moves along behind his or her team and places the small stone in the hands of one of the players. The captain is careful not to disclose to whom the small stone is given. The captain for Team 1 then commands, "Hands in front!" Team 1 players hold their closed hands out in front of them.

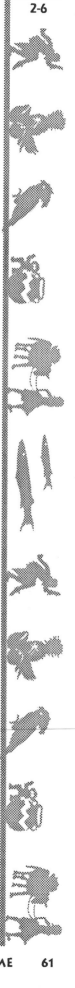

The captain of Team 2 tries to guess which player is holding the small stone. If Team 2's captain guesses correctly, the player holding the small stone hops to the line, gives the small stone to his or her captain, and then hops back to his or her place in the line. A player from Team 2 hops to the large stone and moves the team's large stone a foot farther along the line between the players. The captain of Team 1 places the small stone in the hand of one of his or her teammates as before. The captain of Team 2 continues to guess until he or she misses. When the captain misses a guess, the other team plays. The object of the game is to see which team can move the large stone the farthest. Each time a team begins a new turn, a new captain is designated.

THUMPER

DOMINICAN REPUBLIC

TYPE

Quiet classroom game

SOMETHING ABOUT THE COUNTRY

Music and dance is a large part of life in the Dominican Republic, just as it is in the United States. The "Meringue" is the national dance of the Dominican Republic. The music has African and Spanish influences and is performed by all ages. This dance is also done in countries in Central America.

EQUIPMENT

None

FORMATION

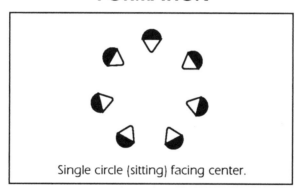

Single circle (sitting) facing center.

DESCRIPTION

Each player selects a one-handed sign or signal that is different from any other player's sign and shows it to the group. For example, one player might make a "V" sign by holding up two fingers. Another player might decide to place a hand on his or her shoulder. Each player uses one hand to thump on the floor to help keep a rhythm set by the leader.

The leader then starts the game by using the free hand to make his or her own sign and then that of another player. The player who was just signaled by the leader, must immediately repeat his or her own sign and then make a third player's sign. The game continues back and forth across and around the circle. If a player is unable to keep the rhythm or respond with a hand sign, he or she receives a consequence designated by the other players. The consequence might be to drink a glass of water, eat dry crackers, or simply keep account of the number of misses of other players. The player with the fewest misses at the end of the playing time is declared the winner.

LIMBO ROCK

WEST INDIES

BACKGROUND

Wonderful music and Limbo dancing are an enchanting tradition in the West Indies. Originally for men only, everyone can Limbo with a bit of flexibility. To Limbo, the dancer bends backwards under a horizontal pole. The dancer must get under the pole using shuffling hops without touching the pole in any way. After each turn, the bar is lowered.

MUSIC (4/4)

"Limbo," Children's All-Time Rhythm Favorites 630, Educational Activities or "Caribbean Mixer," 1523, Folkraft.

FORMATION

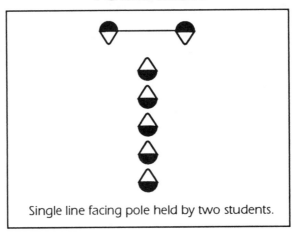

Single line facing pole held by two students.

Each child in turn advances and moves under the pole, leaning backwards without touching the pole or the floor. (Begin with the pole high enough so that each dancer succeeds the first few times.) After each dancer has had a turn, lower the height of the pole. Continue lowering the pole to add challenge and excitement.

VARIATIONS AND SUGGESTIONS

Caribbean Two-Step

For a definition of the two-step, see page 226.

Approach the pole with a two-step. Step forward on L, touch R ball of foot beside L, step forward on L (2 cts).

    Step forward on R, touch L ball of foot beside R, step forward on R (2 cts).

Beguine Step

    Approach the pole by shuffling feet sideways LRL and RLR while rocking hips at the same time.

Body Movements

    Invite more mature dancers to move under the pole on both feet, flexing shoulders and arms.

LIMBO ROCK MIXER

WEST INDIES

BACKGROUND

The West Indies are a chain of tropical islands separating the Atlantic Ocean from the Caribbean Sea. Some of the better-known islands are Cuba, Dominican Republic, Haiti, the Bahamas, Jamaica, Barbados, Puerto Rico, and the Virgin Islands.

This version of the Limbo Rock Mixer is based upon patterns learned from Katherine Dunham. She received a fellowship to study dance and culture in the West Indies and through her studies became an authority on the dances of the region.

MUSIC (2/4)

"Limbo Rock" or flipside "Panamanian Tambour," 1523, Folkraft or "Dance Merengue," Going Places 644, Educational Activities.

FORMATION

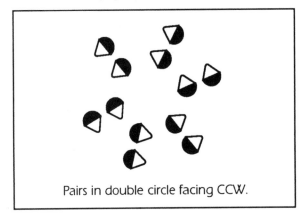

Pairs in double circle facing CCW.

COUNTS	STEPS
16	**1. Caribbean Two-Step** For a definition of the two-step, see page 226. Moving CCW, step forward on flat of L, step on ball of R beside L , and step forward on L (2 cts). Moving CCW, step forward on flat of R, step on ball of L beside R, step forward on R (2 cts). Repeat two-steps LRL, RLR, LRL, RLR, LRL, RLR (12 cts). On the eighth two-step, make a 1/4 turn R (RLR) to face out, backs to center.

8

2. Heel-Toe/Pivot on Two-Step

With backs to center, extend L heel forward while
leaning backward and then extend L toe backward
while leaning forward (2 cts).

Pivot L 1/2 turn with a two-step LRL (2 cts).

Facing center, extend R heel forward while leaning
backward, and then extend R toe backward (2 cts).

Pivot R 1/4 turn to face CCW with a two-step RLR (2 cts).

8

3. Cross Step Sideways R-L

For a definition of the cross step, see page 225.

Facing CCW and moving away from center, step L across
R (1 ct), step sideways R on ball of R foot (count "1
and").

Repeat three more times moving sideways R (count "2,
and, 3, and, 4 and"). Bring R toe by L ankle on final
step to prepare to move sideways L.

Facing CCW and moving toward center, repeat cross
steps stepping L across R (4 cts). End with L toe by R
ankle.

VARIATIONS AND SUGGESTIONS

Mixer

Inside partner moves forward on series of two-steps in Step 1 or
advances diagonally forward on second set of cross steps in Step 3.

Two-Step

The two-step has a "down-up-down" feeling. Head, arms, shoulders,
hips, and knees are all active. Practice until the action is smooth and easy.
Body and arms may swing or sway with the feet, or arms may swing forward
and backward in opposition to foot that is forward. For a definition of the
two-step, see page 226.

Cross Step

The cross step has the feeling of a "Buzz" step. Cue the step by saying,
"Cross-toe, cross-toe, cross-toe, change." For a definition of the "Buzz" step
and the cross step, see page 225.

Rhythm

The African influence is an essential component in Caribbean dancing.
It is pelvic-centered and has a light, buoyant, rhythmic quality.

 MANEE GOGO

WEST INDIES

BACKGROUND

This action song and dance is brimming with authentic West Indies style and instrumentation. Invite dancers to sing while they move, as the words of the song key the action. The framework of the dance provides movement options, making the dance available to all levels.

MUSIC (4/4)

"Manee Gogo," Rainy Day Activities 553, Educational Activities.

FORMATION

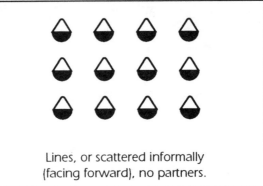

Lines, or scattered informally
(facing forward), no partners.

COUNTS	STEPS
16	Introduction (wait in place)
16	**1. Chorus: Step with Your Feet** Step on alternate flat feet in place while flexing knees. Or, extend L foot sideways and step on L beside R. Extend R foot sideways and step on R beside L. Continue for the full count.
16	**2. Shake Hands and Jump About** Bounce freely side to side, forward-backward, or turning. Shake hands while bouncing. Or, do a simple "rope jump."
8	**3. Interlude** Pump or seesaw bent elbows (6 cts) and clap three quick claps (2 cts).
16	**4. Chorus: Step with Your Feet** Repeat Step 1.

16 **5. Squat Down Low/Stand**
Squat and move freely about. Or, stand and extend one leg and then the other. Or, squat and extend legs forward or sideways.

8 **6. Interlude**
Repeat Step 3.

16 **7. Chorus: Step with Your Feet**
Repeat Step 1.

16 **8. Hop About**
Hop freely on alternate feet moving freely about. Or, hop on one foot and tap other beside it.

8 **9. Interlude**
Repeat Step 3.

16 **10. Chorus: Step with Your Feet**
Repeat Step 1.

16 **11. Twist About**
Twist freely in place. May twist moving down and up.

8 **12. Interlude**
Repeat Step 3.

16 **13. Chorus: Step with Your Feet**
Repeat Step 1.

VARIATIONS AND SUGGESTIONS

Creative Movement
Invite dancers to design their own interlude actions.

Partner Dance/Mixer
Partners (facing each other) scatter informally. On the interlude, each dancer can move to a new partner.

CENTRAL AMERICA

GAMES AND DANCES

Mexico

Guatemala

El Salvador

RIMA DE GALLOS (THE COCK FIGHT)

MEXICO

TYPE

Active classroom game

SOMETHING ABOUT THE COUNTRY

Sports, or deportes, in Mexico are almost art forms. Bullfighting, soccer, jai alai, and horseracing are all very popular.

EQUIPMENT

✓Construction paper or felt pieces of various colors
✓Safety pins

FORMATION

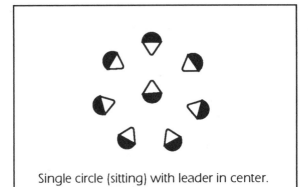

Single circle (sitting) with leader in center.

DESCRIPTION

This is an excellent game for reinforcing Spanish color words, such as rojo (red), azul (blue), verde (green), negro (black), amarillo (yellow), and so on. The leader chooses two players to be the cocks. The players who pretend to be cocks stand with their backs to the leader while the leader pins a piece of colored paper or felt on their backs. (Each player should have a different color.) The two players stand facing each other inside the circle. On a given signal, each player tries to discover the color of the paper or felt·on the back of his or her opponent by moving or jumping around without letting the opponent see his or her own color. Players may not touch each other. The first player to call out correctly the Spanish name of the color on the back of his or her opponent is the winner. The leader then picks two more players and the game continues.

ANDARES-ANDARES

GUATEMALA

TYPE

Active classroom or playground game

SOMETHING ABOUT THE COUNTRY

Like many other countries in Central America, religion is an important aspect of life in Guatemala. The church is the most prominent landmark in Guatemalan villages. The village square faces the church, while other businesses and buildings border the square.

EQUIPMENT

None

FORMATION

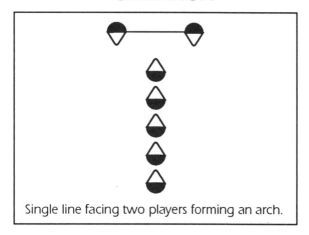

Single line facing two players forming an arch.

DESCRIPTION

This game is best played with ten or twelve players. The two players forming the arch each assume a name, such as Rose and Lily. Players forming the chain pass under the arch (the doors). At the beginning of the game only, the doors ask the player at the head of the chain:

Q. What did he tell you, Andares?
A. To let me pass.
Q. The doors are broken.
A. Send them to repair.
Q. With what money?
A. With little white eggshells.
Q. Where do you find that money?
A. In little boards and big boards.
Q. Where is the money kept?
A. In little bags and in big bags.

Q. What do you give me if I let you pass?

A. The little donkey that comes behind, if she lets you catch her.

Spanish Translation

Q. ¿Qué te dijo, Andares?

A. Que me dejaras pasar.

Q. Están las puertas quebradas.

A. Mandalas a componer.

Q. ¿Con qué dinero?

A. Con cascaritas de huevo güero.

Q. ¿Dónde se encuentra ese dinero?

A. En tabilitas y en tablones.

Q. ¿Dónde se guarda ese dinero?

A. En bolsitas y en bolsones.

Q. ¿Qué me das de prenda si te dejo pasar?

A. La burriquita que viene atrás, si acaso se deja agarrar.

The chain passes under the arch and the two arch players (Rose and Lily) try to catch the last link of the chain by lowering their arms. (You may want to play music as the players pass under the arch. Then the arch lowers their arms and catches a player when the music stops.) When they do, the arch players ask the caught player, "With whom do you want to go, Rose or Lily?" The player whispers the choice to the arch players who then direct the player to stand behind either Rose or Lily. (Players forming the chain are unaware of which arch player has which name. This way, players cannot show a preference for which team they will end up on as the game continues.) Remaining players continue to pass in the same manner.

When all players have been caught, each arch player will be the head of a new chain. Chain members hold the waist of the player in front of them and arch players hold hands. Players from both sides pull like a tug-of-war. The chain that does not break is the winning team. Arch players change names in secret at the start of each new game.

EL PERIQUITO (THE LITTLE PARROT)

MEXICO

TYPE

Quiet classroom game

SOMETHING ABOUT THE COUNTRY

There are many species of parrots that live in warm climates around the world. Macaws are the most common in Central America, with bright, colorful feathers and tails. Parrots and other colorful birds, exotic animals, and tropical plants flourish in the lush rain forests of Mexico.

EQUIPMENT

✓Small object, such as a stone, beanbag, or eraser

FORMATION

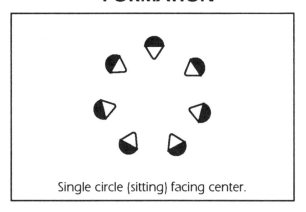

Single circle (sitting) facing center.

DESCRIPTION

Choose one player to begin the game. This player holds the small object in his or her hand. The player turns to the player on the R and says very seriously "Won't you buy this little parrot?" The other asks "Does it bite?" The first answers "No, it does not bite." Then the first player gives the object to the player on the R. The new owner turns to the player on his or her R and asks the same question. When the second player is asked if the parrot bites, he or she must turn back to the first player and ask "Does it bite?" When the second player receives the answer, "No, it does not bite," he or she repeats this to the third player and gives the object to him or her.

The game goes on in this way with the question "Does it bite?" always being referred back from player to player, around the circle, to the first player for the answer. The answer is likewise passed from player to player back to the player who then holds the object. The player who forgets to pass along the dialogue or who laughs must pay a forfeit (see page 9). For added fun, pass another object around the circle at the same time, but in the opposite direction.

PIN

GUATEMALA

TYPE

Quiet classroom or playground game

SOMETHING ABOUT THE COUNTRY

Guatemalans are well-known for their colorful weavings. The intricate designs and choice of colors are unique to each area of the country. Traditionally, the patterns and designs of each weaving read like a book, telling about the weaver's home, tribe, and language.

EQUIPMENT

✓Milk cartons or cones (one per group)
✓Rubber balls (two per group)

FORMATION

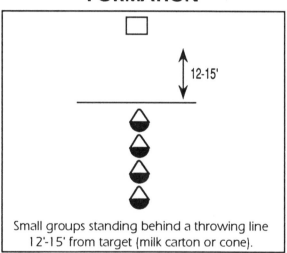

Small groups standing behind a throwing line
12'-15' from target (milk carton or cone).

DESCRIPTION

Players stand behind the throwing line. The first player rolls the first ball toward the milk carton or cone (pin). Players, in turn, each roll the other ball toward the first ball, trying to move the first ball close enough to touch the pin without knocking it over. Each player, following his or her throw, retrieves the ball and brings it back to the throwing line for the next player. The game ends when the first ball touches the pin. If the pin is knocked over, a new game is begun. Groups can compete against each other by keeping track of how many rolls it takes their team to hit the target.

EL GAVILÁN, LA CONEJA, Y LOS CONEJOS (THE HAWK AND THE RABBITS)

EL SALVADOR

TYPE

Active playground game

SOMETHING ABOUT THE COUNTRY

Using the same techniques as their ancestors, Salvadorans create beautiful weavings. Certain villages specialize in weaving a specific item, such as hammocks, mats, or hats. Villages are known for the specific products they weave.

EQUIPMENT

None

FORMATION

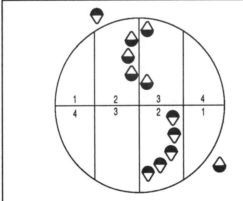

A circle is marked in a play area and divided in half. Each half is sectioned off into four parts. Two equal teams each form a column and stand in one half of the circle. Two gaviláns are outside the circle. The two teams do not interact.

DESCRIPTION

Players on each team stand in a column behind one player chosen as the coneja (mother rabbit). The other players are the conejos (rabbits). Rabbits grasp each other by the waist. The gaviláns enter the circle and try to catch the last rabbit in each line. The rabbits keep moving away behind the coneja, while the gavilán and coneja always remain face to face.

The coneja protects the rabbits with open arms. When a gavilán seizes the last rabbit, a corresponding number of rabbits are carried away as the number of the zone where the catch takes place. For example, if a gavilán catches the last rabbit in zone 3, he or she carries away three rabbits. The gavilán continues trying to catch the rabbits for a specific time limit (usually 10 minutes). Rabbits who are left when the time has expired are the next gaviláns. The rabbits cannot leave their half of the circle. If a gavilán is touched by the coneja, the gavilán must leave the circle and start again.

MEXICAN CLAP DANCE

MEXICO

BACKGROUND

Festivals are a major part of the Mexican way of life. Festivals are made up of dancing, music, fireworks, parades, piñatas, and so on. There are special feast days for many of the saints. The cities and villages participate in these celebrations, but the celebrations are more traditional in rural areas. This popular Mexican folk dance is composed of simple and basic steps.

MUSIC (3/4)

"The Mexican Clap Dance," Dances Without Partners 32, Educational Activities.

FORMATION

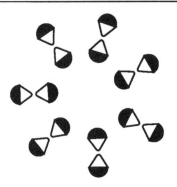

Pairs in double circle facing each other
(inside partner's back to center). Inside partner clasps
hands in back. Outside partner clasps hands in front.

COUNTS	STEPS
12	Introduction (wait in place)
48	**1. Heel Toe-Toe/Stamp-Clap-Clap**

1. Heel Toe-Toe/Stamp-Clap-Clap

Inside partner steps forward on L heel (1 ct), pushes back on R ball of foot in place (1 ct), steps on ball of L beside R (1 ct).

Same partner steps forward on R heel, pushes back on L ball of foot in place, steps on ball of R beside L (3 cts).

In place, same partner stamps L and holds (3 cts), then claps twice quickly (3 cts). (The claps are in time with the claps on the record.)

Repeat Step 1 three more times (36 cts).

(Outside partner does same steps on opposite foot.)

2. Mexican Waltz (Flat-Toe-Toe)

For a definition of the waltz, see page 226.

Inside partner steps directly backward on L,
steps on ball of R beside L, steps on ball of L in
place (3 cts).

Same partner steps directly backward on R,
steps on ball of L beside R, steps on ball of R
in place (3 cts).

Repeat flat-toe-toe series (6 cts).

Moving forward, steps as LRL, RLR, LRL, RLR with
flat-toe-toe waltz steps (12 cts).

Repeat Step 2 (24 cts). Inside partner veers
forward L to meet a new partner stepping
LRL, RLR and stamp-clap-clap.

(Outside partner does same steps on opposite
foot.)

VARIATIONS AND SUGGESTIONS

Step 1

Make one complete turn to the L, stepping LRL and RLR. In place, stamp
L-clap-clap.

Make one complete turn to the R, stepping RLR and LRL. In place, stamp
R-clap-clap.

Step 2

Step Swing Waltz

Step backward on L and swing R across L (3 cts).
Step backward on R and swing L across R (3 cts).
Continue for the full count.

Mexican Waltz (with a Hesitation)

Step backward on L, touch R beside L, and hold (3 cts).
Step backward on R, touch L beside R, and hold (3 cts).
Continue for the full count.

This is an authentic Mexican style and the easiest waltz step.

Formation

Do the dance in lines without partners, or with partners, side by side in
lines rather than in a double circle.

LA CUCARACHA

MEXICO

BACKGROUND

Spicy Mexican food is very popular in the United States. Americans are most familiar with tacos, tamales, and enchiladas, but there are many other native Mexican foods that are not as well-known among non-Mexicans, such as mole, a sauce made from chocolate, nuts, and hot spices served with chicken or turkey. La Cucaracha (koo-ka-RA-cha) is a favorite song and dance in Mexico and has been equally well-known in this country for many years. This version is "muy Mexicano y muy facil" (very Mexican and very easy)!

MUSIC (3/4)

"La Cucaracha," 1458, Folkraft.

FORMATION

Pairs in double circle facing CCW.
Inside partner clasps hands in back.
Outside partner clasps hands in front.

COUNTS	STEPS
6	Introduction (wait in place)
6	**1. Basic Jarabe** For a definition of the jarabe, see page 225. Inside partner steps forward on L heel, steps on R ball of foot in place, brings ball of L beside R (3 cts). Same partner steps forward on R heel, steps on L ball of foot in place, brings ball of R beside L (3 cts). (Outside partner does same steps on opposite foot.)
6	**2. Stamps** In place, inside partner stamps feet LRLR and holds. (Outside partner does same steps on opposite foot.)

36   **3. Basic Jarabe/Stamps**

Repeat Steps 1 and 2 three more times.

24   **4. Diamond Pattern (Away and Together)**

Moving diagonally forward L, inside partner takes three running steps (LRL) while outside partner, moving diagonally forward R, takes three running steps (RLR). Partners move away from each other.

Facing partner, inside partner stamps R heel twice and holds while outside partner stamps L heel twice and holds (3 cts).

Moving diagonally forward R, inside partner takes three running steps (RLR) while outside partner, moving diagonally forward L, takes three running steps (LRL). Partners move towards each other.

Facing partner, both stamp heel twice and hold.

Repeat Step 4 (12 cts).

24   **5. Waltz Balance and Stamps**

For a definition of the waltz balance, see page 226.

Inside partner steps sideways on L, steps on ball of R beside L, and holds (3 cts).

Same partner steps sideways on R, steps on ball of L beside R, and holds (3 cts).

Same partner stamps in place LRLR and holds (6 cts).

Outside partner does same steps on opposite foot (balancing R then L and stamping RLRL).

Repeat Step 5 (12 cts).

LINDA MUJER

MEXICO

BACKGROUND

Dance fads come and go, but the Linda Mujer (LIN-da moo-HAIR) is one of the "golden oldie" rumbas that has survived the passage of time. While it continues to be popular in Latin America, it shares equal popularity worldwide. The subtle hip movements show the African influence mingled with other cultural influences of the Caribbean. Using any medium-tempo rumba, the basic patterns of this recreational mixer are easy and fun.

MUSIC (4/4)

"Uno, Dos, Tres," Dances Without Partners 32, Educational Activities, or other rumbas, such as "Green Eyes" and "Quizas."

FORMATION

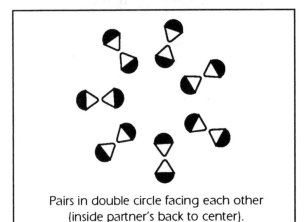

Pairs in double circle facing each other
(inside partner's back to center).

COUNTS	STEPS
16	Introduction (wait in place)
16	**1. Basic Rumba Sideways** Moving sideways L, inside partner steps LRL and touches R beside L (4 cts). Moving sideways R, same partner steps RLR and touches L beside R (4 cts). Repeat steps to R and L (8 cts). (Outside partner does same steps in opposite direction moving R first and then L.) Partners may hold two hands, or dance with hands free.

16   **2. Get Down**

For a definition of the get down step, see page 227.

Inside partner steps forward on L (short step), steps on R in place, steps on L beside R, and steps on R in place (4 cts).

At the same time, outside partner steps backward on R (short step), steps on L in place, steps on R beside L, and steps on L in place.

Repeat three more times (12 cts).

16   **3. Star R (Rumba Walk)**

For a definition of the star R or L, see page 226.

Partners join R hands with elbows bent and forearms adjacent and turn once around CW in place with four "threes." Inside partner steps LRL hold, RLR hold, LRL hold, RLR hold.

Outside partner steps RLR hold, LRL hold, RLR hold, LRL hold.

16   **4. Threes Away and Progress**

Moving backward, inside partner steps LRL hold and RLR hold while outside partner backs away, stepping RLR hold and LRL hold (8 cts).

Inside partner veers forward to the R to a new partner, stepping LRL hold and RLR hold, while outside partner veers forward to his or her L, stepping RLR hold and LRL hold (8 cts).

VARIATIONS AND SUGGESTIONS

Step 1: Back Break

For a definition of the back break, see page 225.

Inside partner steps backward on L, steps on R in place, steps on L beside R, and holds (4 cts). Same partner steps backward on R, steps on L in place, steps on R beside L, and holds (4 cts).

Repeat all (8 cts).

(At the same time, outside partner breaks backward also, but begins on R.)

Step 2: Side Break

For a definition of the side break, see page 225.

Inside partner steps sideways on L (short step), steps on R in place, steps on L beside R, and steps on R in place (4 cts).

(At the same time, outside partner does same steps, but breaks to the R.)

Step 3

Do the turn with R hips adjacent rather than holding hands in a star.

Step 4

Moving backward, inside partner steps L and R (slow, slow) and then LRL (quick, quick, slow) 8 cts. Moving forward, inside partner steps R and L (slow, slow) and RLR (quick, quick, slow) 8 cts.

(Outside partner does the same steps, but veers to his or her L when progressing.)

Formation

Do the dance without partners or with partners side by side in lines rather than in a double circle.

LET'S CHA CHA
MEXICO

BACKGROUND

For 300 years, Mexico existed under Spanish rule with its language, religion, and laws. On September 16, 1810, Mexico began its fight for independence. Eleven years later, in 1821, freedom was proclaimed. Today, there remains a strong Spanish influence throughout Mexico. September 16 is one of Mexico's most exciting festivals.

The Cha Cha has remained a popular social dance worldwide along with the Rumba, Mambo, Samba, and Tango. This dance may be done solo, with a partner, or as a mixer.

MUSIC (4/4)

"Let's Cha Cha," Dances Without Partners 33, Educational Activities.

FORMATION

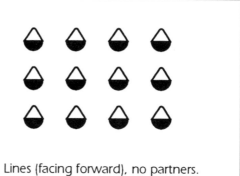

Lines (facing forward), no partners.

COUNTS	STEPS
16	Introduction (wait in place)
16	**1. Basic Cha Cha** Step forward on L (1 ct), step back on R in place (1 ct), move slightly backward stepping LRL (2 cts). Step backward on R, step forward on L, move slightly forward stepping RLR (4 cts). Repeat Step 1 (8 cts).
16	**2. Step-Closes** Moving sideways L, step on L, close R, step on L, close R (4 cts). Step sideways on L (2 cts) and close R (2 cts).

Moving sideways R, step on R, close L, step on R, close L (4 cts).

Step sideways on R (2 cts) and close L (2 cts).

Cue the step by saying, "Step-close step-close, step and close."

16

3. Mambo Break

For a definition of breaks, see page 225.

Step forward on L, step in place on R, bring L to R and hold (4 cts).

Step backward on R, step in place on L, bring R to L and hold (4 cts).

Repeat (8 cts).

16

4. Step-Step, Clap-Clap

In place, step L and R and then clap twice (4 cts).

Repeat three more times (12 cts).

VARIATIONS AND SUGGESTIONS

Partner Dance

Partners in double circle face each other (inside partner's back to center). Steps are all the same, except outside partner will do steps on opposite foot.

Mixer

On Step 4, inside partner gradually moves sideways L to meet a new partner.

EL MOSQUITO
MEXICO

BACKGROUND

The music of Mexico is a mixture of many cultures—Spanish, African, Caribbean, Mexican Indian, and more.

This version of El Mosquito, based upon the music of La Mosca (The Fly), has been arranged for all ages.

MUSIC (2/4)

"Mexican Jumping Bean," Dances Without Partners 33, Educational Activities.

FORMATION

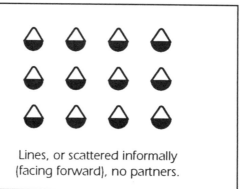

Lines, or scattered informally (facing forward), no partners.

COUNTS	STEPS
8	Introduction (wait in place)

16   **1. Bounce Freely**

With feet together, bounce freely with short bounces side to side, forward and backward, or turning. Flutter or flap arms at the same time. End facing forward.

16   **2. Flap Arms, Close-Open Fingers**

Lean forward and flap bent elbows (2 cts). Straighten body and close and open fingers twice (2 cts).
Repeat flapping arms and closing and opening fingers three more times (12 cts).

16   **3. Bite! Bite! (Pica! Pica!)**

Lean forward from the waist. Poke freely in space with alternate index fingers imitating a mosquito biting. Poke in all directions at a low or high level. Say "Pica, pica . . ."

4. Clapping

Clap hands freely. Clap "tortilla style" — R on L and L on R. (The clapping represents the reaction against the pesky mosquitoes.)

VARIATIONS AND SUGGESTIONS

Step 2

Lean forward and flap bent elbows twice (2 cts).
Straighten and flap bent elbows twice (2 cts).
Repeat three more times (12 cts).

Step 4

Instead of clapping, strike the body freely as if swatting mosquitoes.

LA RASPA
MEXICO

BACKGROUND

The title, La Raspa, comes from the Spanish verb "raspar," which means to slide or scratch. The many variations of this dance make it suitable for all ages. It may be performed solo, with a partner, or as a mixer.

MUSIC (2/4)

"La Raspa y la Botella," Activities for Individualization 49, Educational Activities.

FORMATION

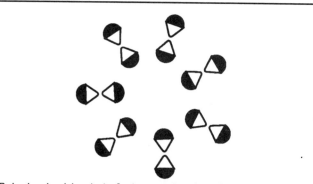

Pairs in double circle facing each other (inside partner's back to center). Inside partner clasps hands in back. Outside partner clasps hands in front.

COUNTS	STEPS
16	Introduction (wait in place)

32

1. La Raspa Shuffle

This step is like a hop.

Step backward on L, extending or sliding R forward (1 ct).

Step backward on R, extending L forward (1 ct).

Step backward on L, extending R forward and hold (2 cts).

Continue shuffle with RLR hold, LRL hold, and so on.

32

2. Skipping Swing

For a definition of the swing, see page 227.

Partners hook R elbows and beginning on R, swing CW 12 skips. Release arms and stamp three times.

Hook L elbows and beginning on L, swing CCW 12 skips. Release arms and stamp three times. Partners end facing each other.

32

3. La Raspa Shuffle/Skipping
Repeat Steps 1 and 2.

32

4. La Raspa Shuffle
Repeat Step 1.

32

5. Jarabe Tapatio
For a definition of the jarabe, see page 225.
Jump apart-together-apart for 12 cts.
End with three stamps and hold (4 cts).
Repeat Step 5 (16 cts).

VARIATIONS AND SUGGESTIONS

Step 1
Add claps at the end of each La Raspa step. RLR clap-clap, LRL clap-clap, and so on.

Mixer
On Step 2, each dancer progresses one place on L, elbow swing to a new partner.

No Partner Dance
Dancers form single circle facing center.

In Step 2, moving CW, all join hands in a big circle. Skip 12 skips, ending with three stamps.

Moving CCW, skip 12 skips CCW and end with three stamps.

La Raspa y la Botella (La Raspa and the Bottle Dance)
Partners face each other. Between them is a "bottle." (For safety, use a small empty milk carton or a small wooden block.)

In Step 2, while one partner does a "show-off" step over or around the bottle (12 cts) and ends with three stamps, the other partner circles CCW with 12 skips and three stamps. The other partner does a "show-off" step (12 cts) and ends with three stamps, while the partner circles CCW with 12 skips and ends with three stamps.

Each dancer may create his or her own "show-off" steps.

EUROPE

GAMES AND DANCES

Iceland

Finland

Sweden

Russia

Scotland

Ireland

Denmark

Lithuania

Holland

England

Germany

Poland

Belgium

Czechoslovakia

France

Hungary

Italy

Switzerland

Yugoslavia

Bulgaria

Spain

Greece

ALLE VOGELS VLIEGEN (ALL THE BIRDS FLY)

HOLLAND

TYPE
Quiet classroom game

SOMETHING ABOUT THE COUNTRY
Holland is well-known for its many water canals and windmills. Traditionally, windmills were built to pump water from the land into the canals. In Holland in the wintertime, you can often see ice-skaters skating to town on frozen canals.

EQUIPMENT
✓Handkerchief

FORMATION

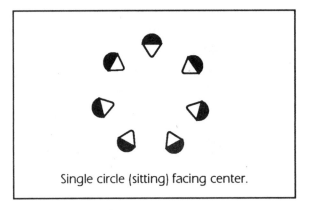

Single circle (sitting) facing center.

DESCRIPTION
Choose one player to be the leader. The leader names some objects that fly and some that do not—one at a time. For example, the leader may say "pigeons fly." Since that is true, players raise both arms as if to fly. But, if for example, the leader says "elephants fly," players keep their arms down. The leader names objects quickly, in order to confuse players. Players who make a mistake must pay a forfeit, or "pand," as it is called in Holland. The game continues until every player has paid at least one forfeit.

The forfeits are piled in the center of the circle and covered with a handkerchief (see "forfeits" on page 9). The leader touches one forfeit through the handkerchief and asks the other players what the child who owns it must do to get it back. The group may suggest such things as singing a song or performing a stunt (see page 223). When the action is done, the player gets his or her forfeit back. All players win their forfeits back in this way.

IN-AND-OUT-THE WINDOWS

ICELAND

TYPE

Active classroom or playground game

SOMETHING ABOUT THE COUNTRY

Iceland is the land of the midnight sun, with light almost 24 hours a day in June. On the opposite side of the calendar, December brings almost 24 hours of darkness. Iceland is warmer than many countries that far north because of the Gulf stream ocean current which flows past Iceland's coast.

EQUIPMENT

✔Music

FORMATION

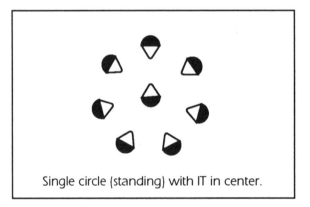

Single circle (standing) with IT in center.

DESCRIPTION

Players join hands in the circle and raise their joined hands above their heads. When the music begins, IT begins to weave his or her way in and out between the raised arms. The moment the music stops, IT steps in front of the player nearest to him or her. That player and IT join hands and, when the music begins again, weave their way in and out of the circle. When the music stops again, the two players stand before two other players. Now, four players, hands joined in a chain-like formation, continue to go in-and-out the windows when the music begins again. The game proceeds in this way until no one is left in the circle.

BATON MAUDIT (THE CURSED STICK)

BELGIUM

TYPE

Active classroom game

SOMETHING ABOUT THE COUNTRY

Belgium has two official languages. The northern people, called Flemings, speak Flemish, which is similar to Dutch. The southern Walloons speak French. A line running east and west, just south of Brussels, divides the country into the two regions.

EQUIPMENT

✓Stick, short dowel, or rolled newspaper
✓Blindfold

FORMATION

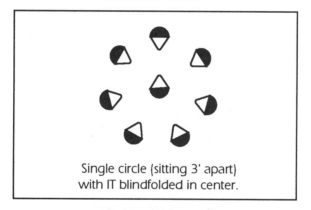

Single circle (sitting 3' apart)
with IT blindfolded in center.

DESCRIPTION

To begin Baton Maudit (ba-TAWN mow-DEE), players pass the stick to one another around the circle. When the blindfolded player whistles, the player caught holding the stick must perform a silly stunt, such as a forward roll, singing a song, or saying a tongue twister. Remind players that they may not throw the stick to the next player to avoid being caught holding it. The stick must be passed.

NORTH WINDS AND THE SOUTH WIND

SWEDEN

TYPE
Active playground game

SOMETHING ABOUT THE COUNTRY
In the last week of June, Sweden holds a celebration of Midsummer Eve when the sun shines almost around the clock. During this celebration of the return of summer, Swedes dance around a tall wooden pole decorated with leaves and wild flowers, much like our Maypole celebration.

EQUIPMENT
✓Ribbons (2 blue and 1 yellow)
✓Safety pins

FORMATION

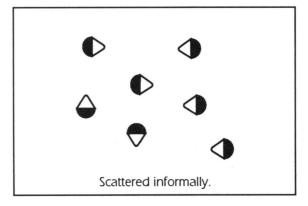

Scattered informally.

DESCRIPTION
The two players chosen to represent the North Winds wear blue ribbons. The player chosen to represent the South Wind wears a yellow ribbon. The North Winds are cold and dangerous. They run around the play area trying to tag as many players as possible. When tagged by the North Wind, a player squats down on all fours and becomes stiff and motionless. The South Wind attempts to free as many players as possible by tagging them and shouting "free." Players tagged by the South Wind are brought back to life and take part in the game again. After a determined length of time, the players not freed by the South Wind are counted. If there are five or fewer, the South Wind wins. If there are more than five, the North Winds win.

SARVISILLA

FINLAND

TYPE

Quiet classroom game

SOMETHING ABOUT THE COUNTRY

A sauna, which means "dry heat bath" in Finnish, is one of Finland's oldest traditions. A sauna consists of a small wooden cabin where water is poured over hot stones inside to produce steam. Saunas are used for relaxation by both children and adults. It's estimated that there are as many as one million saunas in Finland.

EQUIPMENT

None

FORMATION

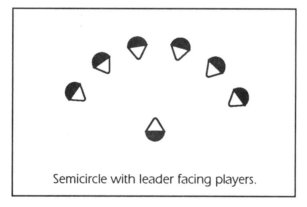

Semicircle with leader facing players.

DESCRIPTION

The leader, known as the "horner," says "Horns, horns, horns—buckhorns." Players then spread their fingers and place hands (palms forward) on each side of their head like horns. But if the leader says (for example) "Horns, horns, horns—dog horns," players put their hands down. Players who lift their hands to their heads when the animal mentioned has no horns must pay a forfeit (see page 9). Players must also pay a forfeit (pantti) if they do not lift their fingers to make horns when they should or are too slow in making the horns. In order to collect more forfeits, the leader can make horns with his or her fingers when it is not appropriate to deceive the other players.

JAK SIE MASZ

POLAND

TYPE
Active playground game

SOMETHING ABOUT THE COUNTRY
Poland means "land of fields." Poland lies between many other European countries with no natural boundaries or defenses on the east or west, which leaves the country open for warring armies in Europe. The Polish people suffered great loss of human lives during World War II.

EQUIPMENT
None

FORMATION

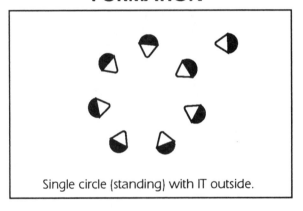

Single circle (standing) with IT outside.

DESCRIPTION
As IT walks around the outside of the circle, he or she taps another player on the shoulder and greets the player saying "dzein dobry" (jane dough-bri) which means "good morning." IT then runs around the circle. The tapped player runs around the circle in the opposite direction. When the two players meet, they shake hands, stoop three times, and say "Jak sie masz?"(Yaak sheh ma-sh?), which means "How are you?" The players then pass each other and continue running around the circle to the vacant spot. The last player to reach the spot becomes IT for the next round and the game continues.

TAG

SPAIN

TYPE
Active playground game

SOMETHING ABOUT THE COUNTRY
If you are a matador or bullfighter in Spain, you are considered a hero. Bullfighting is one of Spain's best known and most unusual spectacles. Most cities throughout Spain have at least one bullring.

EQUIPMENT
None

FORMATION

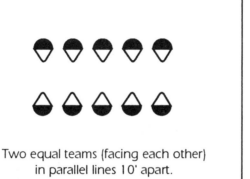

Two equal teams (facing each other)
in parallel lines 10' apart.

DESCRIPTION
One team is named "Seville" and the other "Barcelona." A player from Seville is chosen to travel to Barcelona. All players from Barcelona hold up their L hands, palms facing outward. The player from Seville walks along the Barcelona line, rubbing his or her R palm over the extended palm of each player until finally clapping the palm of one Barcelona player. The Barcelona player then chases the Seville player as he or she races toward the Seville line. If the Barcelona player tags the opponent before he or she reaches the Seville line, the Seville player is taken captive to the Barcelona line. Play continues with a Barcelona player traveling to Seville and repeating the same action. The object is for the citizens of one city to capture all the citizens from the other.

UNWRAP THE CHOCOLATE

GERMANY

TYPE

Quiet classroom game

SOMETHING ABOUT THE COUNTRY

In 1946, Germany was divided into two separate countries—East Germany and West Germany. A wall divided the two Germanys. In 1990, the wall was torn down and Germany and its people were reunited.

EQUIPMENT

✓Chocolate bar wrapped several times in newspaper or brown wrap
✓Scarf
✓Pair of gloves
✓Knife
✓Fork
✓Pair of dice

FORMATION

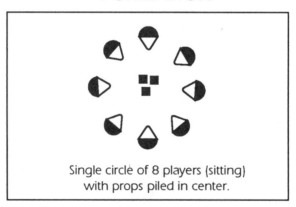

Single circle of 8 players (sitting)
with props piled in center.

DESCRIPTION

Winners of this German game get an immediate reward—a bite of chocolate! Before the game starts, each player rolls the dice. The player rolling the highest number begins the game. Each player in turn rolls the dice. If a double number is not rolled, the player passes the dice on to the player to his or her R. If a player rolls a double number, he or she goes to the center and quickly puts on the gloves and scarf and begins to unwrap the chocolate bar. Meanwhile, the dice are passed on to the next player. The next player who rolls a double number replaces the player currently in the center. The player puts on the gloves and scarf and continues unwrapping the chocolate bar. When the chocolate is unwrapped, players rolling double numbers wear the props and use the knife and fork to cut off a piece of chocolate to eat. Victory may look sweet, but if a player does not actually have the chocolate in his or her mouth when another player rolls a double number, he or she must stop and pass the props on to the new center player.

WEE BOLOGNA MAN

SCOTLAND

TYPE
Quiet classroom game

SOMETHING ABOUT THE COUNTRY
In Scotland, families related to each other through a common ancestor belong to a "clan." The members of each clan elect a chieftain who makes important clan decisions.

EQUIPMENT
None

FORMATION

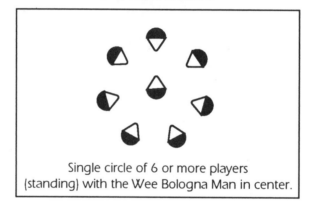

Single circle of 6 or more players
(standing) with the Wee Bologna Man in center.

DESCRIPTION
The player standing in the center of the circle is the Wee Bologna Man who chants:

"I'm the Wee Bologna Man.
Always do the best you can
To follow the Wee Bologna Man."

The Wee Bologna Man then pantomimes an action, such as eating or driving a car. Other players watch closely and copy exactly what the Wee Bologna Man does. The Wee Bologna Man changes actions quickly and frequently to confuse the players who are trying to copy his or her actions. A player who fails to change actions is out or may pay a forfeit and continue to play in the game. Each time a player leaves the circle, the Wee Bologna Man repeats the rhyme faster and changes actions more frequently. When there are only a few players left in the circle, the Wee Bologna Man chooses another player to take his or her place. All players return to the circle and the game begins again. If forfeits are paid, have players redeem them (see page 9) before beginning a new game.

THE WHALES

DENMARK

TYPE

Active classroom game

SOMETHING ABOUT THE COUNTRY

Because of Denmark's proximity to the sea, fishing is important to the livelihood of many Danes. The Danes fish the North Sea, Baltic Sea, and waterways between Denmark, Norway, and Sweden.

EQUIPMENT

✓Slips of paper
✓Pencils

FORMATION

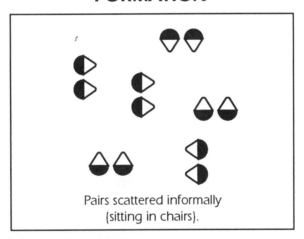

Pairs scattered informally
(sitting in chairs).

DESCRIPTION

The Danish have always been great sailors. This popular game reflects the Danes' interest in the sea. Name one pair of players as the lead pair ("whales"). Other pairs each choose a name of a fish, write it on a slip of paper, and hand it to the whales. The whales begin to walk hand in hand around the room weaving in and out among the pairs' chairs. The whales start to call out the names of the fish on the slips of paper. "Barracuda," they shout, "herring, dolphin and tuna!" Each pair of players rises when their name is called and falls in line behind the whales, still marching around the room. After the whales have called out all the names and every pair is marching around the room, the whales call out, "A storm is coming. Head for home!" All players run for seats. Pairs cannot separate. They must stay in pairs and find seats together. The pair unable to find chairs will be the whales for the next game. Each pair of players can select a new fish name for each new game.

ZMIRKE
YUGOSLAVIA

TYPE
Quiet classroom game

SOMETHING ABOUT THE COUNTRY
Yugoslavia is almost completely covered by mountains, hills, and plateaus. At the time this book went to press, Yugoslavia was in a state of flux. Yugoslavia soon will be divided into separate republics or countries, each with its own borders and government.

EQUIPMENT
✓ Stick
✓ Blindfold

FORMATION

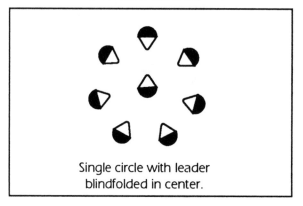

Single circle with leader
blindfolded in center.

DESCRIPTION
Give the blindfolded player the stick. Players in the circle hold hands and sing while circling CW:

Our poor little baby with overbound eyes
Does not see about him the light of the sun.
He shall see it when guessing his fellow,
He shall see it when guessing his fellow.

When the song ends, the blindfolded player strikes the stick on the ground and other players stop circling. The blindfolded player calls "Ye em!" to the player who is directly in front of him or her. This player must reply by saying "Em yel" The player who replies tries to disguise his or her voice in order to deceive the blindfolded player. If the blindfolded player can identify the player who replied, the two exchange places. If the blindfolded player guesses incorrectly, he or she remains in the center.

DREI-MANN HOCH (THREE-MAN DEEP)

SWITZERLAND

TYPE

Active playground game

SOMETHING ABOUT THE COUNTRY

Yodeling is a strong tradition in Switzerland. Swiss mountaineers are famous for their yodeling. Group singing and folk dancing are also traditional pastimes, especially in rural areas. Choral societies hold contests to determine the best singers.

EQUIPMENT

None

FORMATION

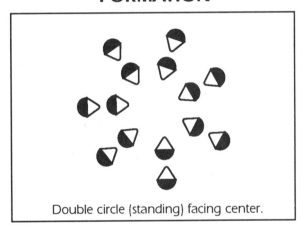

Double circle (standing) facing center.

DESCRIPTION

Choose two players to begin the game. Other players stand in pairs so that one partner is in the inner circle and one partner is directly behind in the outer circle. All of the players face the center. One of the chosen players moves around through the circle while being chased by the other. The player being chased may save himself or herself from being tagged by taking a position in front of (and with his or her back toward) any one of the couples. This unit then becomes the "three-man deep" group. The player at the back of the line then becomes the chased player. If the chased player is caught before saving himself or herself, that player then becomes the new chaser.

IL CUCUZZARO
(THE PUMPKIN PLANTER)

ITALY

TYPE
Quiet classroom game

SOMETHING ABOUT THE COUNTRY
There are many beautiful cities in Italy, but Venice is considered one of the most beautiful. Canals are the main thoroughfares throughout the city. If you call a taxi, it most likely will be a boat!

EQUIPMENT
None

FORMATION

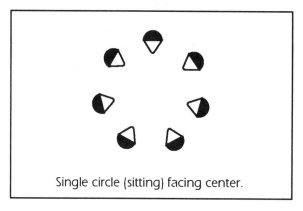

Single circle (sitting) facing center.

DESCRIPTION

Choose one player to be the "Cucuzzaro." The Cucuzzaro gives each player (pumpkin) a number and then stands in the center. The Cucuzzaro begins the dialogue as follows:

Cucuzzaro: "In my orchard there are five pumpkins." (The Cucuzzaro may say any number.)
Pumpkin #5: "Why five pumpkins?"
Cucuzzaro: "If not, how many?"
Pumpkin #5: "Thirteen pumpkins (for example)."

Pumpkin #13 answers the same way and the game goes on faster and faster. If a player forgets to answer quickly or gets confused, he or she must pay a forfeit (see page 9).

PASS THE ORANGE

IRELAND

TYPE

Active classroom game

SOMETHING ABOUT THE COUNTRY

In Ireland, you'll see street signs printed in both Gaelic and English. This is part of an effort by the Irish government to prevent the disappearance of the Gaelic language. Schools in Ireland are also being encouraged to teach Gaelic in addition to English.

EQUIPMENT

✓Oranges (one per team)

FORMATION

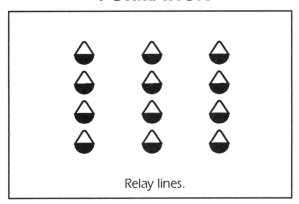

Relay lines.

DESCRIPTION

An orange is most often used in this Irish team game, but any object about the same size that can be passed from chin to chin will do. Give the leader of each team an orange to place under his or her chin. On a given signal, the leaders pass the orange to the next player on their team. Each player must grasp the orange with his or her chin only. No hands or elbows may be used. If an orange is dropped, it must be returned to the leader, who starts the play again. The first team to pass the orange to the end of the line without dropping it wins.

SNAIL WHORL

ENGLAND

TYPE

Active classroom or playground game

SOMETHING ABOUT THE COUNTRY

Soccer is one of the most popular sports in England. Rugby, also popular, is similar to American football without the padding. Cricket is a team sport played with a bat and a ball. The older crowd tends to enjoy lawn bowling.

EQUIPMENT

None

FORMATION

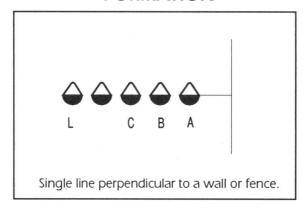

Single line perpendicular to a wall or fence.

DESCRIPTION

All players clasp hands. The player farthest from the wall is the leader (L in diagram). The player closest to the wall (A in diagram) forms an arch by putting a hand against the wall. The leader, followed by the other players, walks hand-in-hand toward the wall and under A's arm. When the last player passes under the arch, player A will be forced to face the opposite direction.

Players repeat the same action, only this time the player next to A (B in diagram) does not go through A's arch, but stands beside A. Players then go between B and A. Since all players are holding hands, player B must cross arms and face in the other direction as player C goes under the arch.

The action is repeated. This time the leader goes between player B and player C. Player C must cross arms and face in the other direction this time around. Action continues until all players are standing with crossed arms facing in the opposite direction. The leader crosses arms as he or she returns to his or her place. Then the leader and player A sidle toward each other and lock elbows forming a circle with all players facing outward, arms crossed. Players whirl around. The leader and player A unlock elbows. Player A goes spinning off as he or she and the player next to him or her uncross arms and unclasp hands. Each player spins off as the circle continues to whirl.

ZEROS
RUSSIA

TYPE
Quiet classroom game

SOMETHING ABOUT THE COUNTRY
Russia is made up of a number of Republics. Cities and regions in Russia and neighboring Republics were at one time barred to outsiders. During the Cold War, as much as 30 percent of the country was off-limits to foreign travelers.

EQUIPMENT
✓Paper
✓Pencils

FORMATION

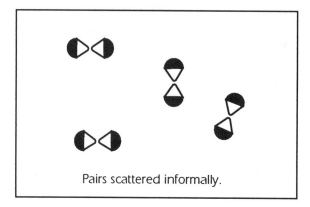

Pairs scattered informally.

DESCRIPTION
Give each pair of players two pencils and a piece of paper with a triangle of zeros (10 across and 10 down) drawn on it.

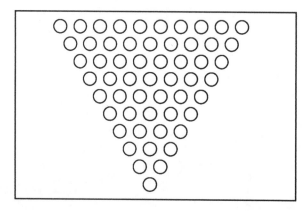

Taking turns, players check off zeros. The object of the game is to check off the last zero in any horizontal or diagonal line. The player who does so receives a score equivalent to the number of zeros in the completed line. Occasionally it will happen that checking off one zero will complete two lines which have the last checked zero in common. In this case, the player's score equals the numerical values of both lines. The zeros at the three corners of the triangle do not constitute lines of one. When all zeros are checked, the player with the highest score wins.

ZPOVED (CONFESSIONS)

CZECHOSLOVAKIA

TYPE
Quiet classroom game

SOMETHING ABOUT THE COUNTRY
Czechoslovakia has a rich tradition of dyeing Easter eggs in beautiful designs. Artists use hot wax to draw the designs on the eggs and then dye the eggs and wax them again. The procedure is repeated until the desired design is completed. The egg is then heated until the wax melts and can be wiped off, leaving an intricate design. At the time this book went to press, Czechoslovakia was in a state of flux. The country will probably be divided into two countries, each with its own borders and government.

EQUIPMENT
None

FORMATION

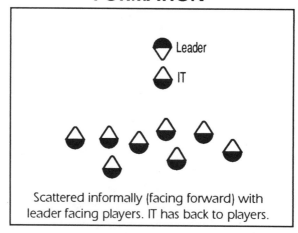

Scattered informally (facing forward) with leader facing players. IT has back to players.

DESCRIPTION
The leader faces IT and asks a set number of questions that require only a "yes," "no," "once," or "never" answer. The leader says aloud only part of the question, acting out the other part so that the players can see him or her. The questions and acting should be humorous, such as "Do you do this every day (acting out washing your face)?" or "How often do you do this (acting out brushing your teeth)?" The idea is to make the questions, motions, and answers as ridiculous as possible. All players should have a turn to answer questions.

SWAP CHAIRS BY THE NUMBERS

FRANCE

TYPE
Active classroom game

SOMETHING ABOUT THE COUNTRY
The greatest national sporting event in France is the Tour de France bicycle race. Teams from all over the world enter this grueling 1,000-mile race across France through a variety of terrains, including steep mountains.

EQUIPMENT
✓Blindfold

FORMATION

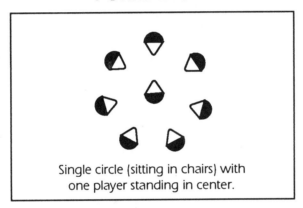

Single circle (sitting in chairs) with
one player standing in center.

DESCRIPTION
This amusing French game is an alternate way to play Blind Man's Bluff, a favorite in some form in many countries of the world. In the French version, all players but one sit in the circle. This player asks children to number off. The number each child calls out is his or her number. Players must remember their numbers throughout the game. After children have numbered off, blindfold the standing player. The blindfolded player calls out two numbers, perhaps 2 and 25. Players with these numbers exchange seats. The object of the game is for the blindfolded player either to tag a player or to find a seat left vacant during an exchange. Players may not go outside the circle, but may walk or crawl as quietly as possible. The blindfolded player takes the number and seat of the player he or she tags or whose chair he or she sits in. The tagged player is then blindfolded and the game continues.

SYLLABLES

GREECE

TYPE

Quiet classroom game

SOMETHING ABOUT THE COUNTRY

There are hundreds of islands that surround Greece. The people who live on these Greek islands are farmers, fishermen, carpenters, boat builders, or own restaurants or inns. The islands are strikingly beautiful, with their wide harbors and white-washed buildings.

EQUIPMENT

✔Bean bag or soft ball

FORMATION

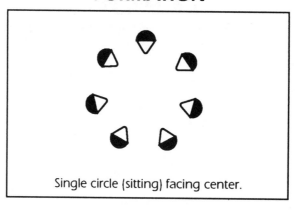

Single circle (sitting) facing center.

DESCRIPTION

Choose one player to be the leader. The leader begins by saying the first syllable of a two-syllable word, such as "win-," and at the same time throwing the bean bag to another player. The player who catches the bean bag must instantly provide the second syllable, such as "-dow," to make the word "window." If the player fails to think of a second syllable, he or she must pay a forfeit and drop out of the game. The last player remaining in the game is the winner. At the end of the game, the winner holds up one forfeit at a time and says "The owner may redeem the forfeit (see page 9) by making the sound of an elephant (or some other animal)," for example.

THE CHILD IS DOWN

SWEDEN

BACKGROUND

The Child Is Down is a singing game based upon an old Swedish tune. Children enjoy the contrast between "sleeping" and bursting into sudden activity. The basic motions that lend themselves to creativity and exploration have made this dance a national hit.

MUSIC (3/4 OR 4/4)

"The Child Is Down," Aerobic Dances For Kids 93, Educational Activities.

FORMATION

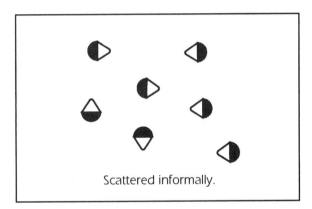

Scattered informally.

WORDS	ACTIONS
Chorus "The child is down, Upon the ground. And sleeps so sound, Like a lazy hound. Ohhhh."	Lie or sit quietly on the floor and pretend to be asleep.
Verse "Get up and do some chopping Get up and chop around." (Repeat.)	Jump up quickly and do some chopping.
"Oh no, the child is down!"	Yawn and lie down again.

VARIATIONS AND SUGGESTIONS

Words

Verses include various activities, such as sweeping, scrubbing, raking, and painting. Work-activity pantomimes may be done in place or moving about.

Creative Movement

Learn the song and create your own words on a cassette tape.

CHIMES OF DUNKIRK

FRANCE AND BELGIUM

BACKGROUND

The Chimes of Dunkirk ("Carillon de Dunkirque") is one of the older traditional folk dances for children. This dance is spirited and yet has a calming quality dancers enjoy. This dance comes from the coastal region of France where the famous evacuation of World War II British troops took place. The music tells us of the age-old church chimes ringing out in the town of Dunkirk.

MUSIC (2/4)

"Chimes of Dunkirk," 1159, Folkraft.

FORMATION

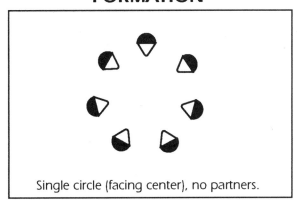

Single circle (facing center), no partners.

COUNTS	STEPS
8	Introduction (wait in place)
8	**1. Stamp and Clap** In place, stamp feet LRL, hold (4 cts). Clap own hands three times, hold (4 cts).
8	**2. Walk Forward-Backward** Walk forward 4 steps, LRLR and backward 4 steps, LRLR.
16	**3. Chorus: Skipping** Join hands and circle L (CW) with 16 skipping steps while singing "Tra, la, la, la."

VARIATIONS AND SUGGESTIONS

Step 2

Swing bent arms down-up representing church bells. Or, extend arms overhead and sway side to side. Or, swing arms forward-backward.

Step 3

Use other basic movements, such as running, galloping, or sliding.

Mixer

Partners (facing each other) scatter informally.

Step 1: Same

Step 2: Slap own thighs twice, clap own hands twice, clap hands of partner three times at chest level and hold (8 cts).

Step 3: Partners join hands and swing CW in place with 8 skips (8 cts). Each dancer then takes 8 walks or skips seeking a new partner to repeat the dance (8 cts). For a definition of the swing, see page 227.

Hand Jive

Dancers are in lines, circles, or scattered with no partners.

Step 1: Same

Step 2: Strike own hands "tortilla" style — R on L, L on R, R on L, and so on (8 cts).

Step 3: Touch toes-knees-hips and clap (4 cts).
Repeat three more times (12 cts).
Or, touch head-shoulders-hips and clap (16 cts).

Stick Game

Pairs in double circle face each other (inside partner's back to center). Each dancer holds two rhythm sticks.

Step 1: Stamp three times, hold and then strike own sticks three times, hold (8 cts).

Step 2: Partners strike R sticks together and then strike own sticks (2 cts).
Partners strike L sticks together and then strike own sticks (2 cts).
Continue alternating for a total of 8 cts.

Step 3: Walk backward four steps while striking sticks with each step (4 cts).
Walk forward four steps while striking sticks (4 cts).
Repeat backward-forward steps (8 cts).
Inside partner may progress forward to new partners on the last set of forward steps.

LITTLE IRISH DANCE

IRELAND

BACKGROUND

Wherever the Irish live, Irish folk music is popular. In addition to their spirited dances and jigs, Irish songs tell of love, sorrow, and a longing for home. The spritely Irish music and easy patterns create a special invitation for children to dance.

MUSIC (6/8)

"Little Irish Dance," Rainy Day Activities 553, Educational Activities, or "Haymaker's Jig," N-4515B, National Records.

FORMATION

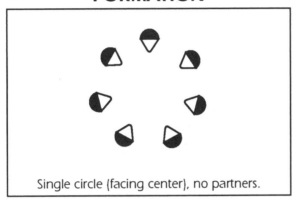

Single circle (facing center), no partners.

COUNTS	STEPS
8	Introduction (wait in place)
32	**1. March in Place and Clap** Step in place LRLR and then clap four times (8 cts). Repeat three more times.
16	**2. Jumping** Beginning with feet together, jump apart, jump together, jump and extend R heel forward, and jump, bringing feet together (4 cts). Repeat three more times.
16	**3. Walk and Skip** Moving CCW, take eight walks and then eight skips around the circle.

VARIATIONS AND SUGGESTIONS

Partner Dance

Partners in double circle face each other (inside partner's back to center).

Step 1: Same (inside partner begins on L, outside partner begins on R)

Step 2: Same

Step 3: Moving backward, take four steps LRLR (4 cts).

Moving forward, take four steps LRLR (4 cts).

Repeat forward and backward steps (8 cts).

Inside partners may veer L on forward steps to meet new partners.

Singing Game

Dancers are scattered, no partners.

Step 1: Dancers skip freely (or move using other basic movements) for 32 counts while singing:

"Uptown, downtown, all around the busy town,
Uptown, downtown, heads say 'Hello.'
Uptown, downtown, all around the busy town,
Uptown, downtown, heads say 'Hello.'"

(On the last line, each dancer stops to meet someone and says "Hello.")

Steps 2 and 3: In small groups, dancers explore ways to say "hello" with head movements for 32 counts while singing:

"Hello, hello, heads say 'hello,'
Hello, hello, we're in the show.
Hello, hello, heads say 'hello,'
Hello, hello, walking we'll go."

The last line indicates how dancers will begin moving (jumping, galloping, sliding) as the dance repeats.

POP GOES THE WEASEL

ENGLAND

BACKGROUND

The English hold a special fondness for the Royal Family and associated traditions. One such tradition is that seven ravens must always live at the Tower of London or the government will fall apart.

MUSIC (6/8)

"Pop Goes the Weasel," Dances Without Partners 33, Educational Activities.

FORMATION

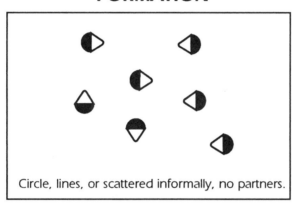

Circle, lines, or scattered informally, no partners.

COUNTS	STEPS
Chord	Introduction (wait in place)
16	**1. Skip CW/Clap** Take 12 skips CW. "Skip to the left and here we go And that's the way to do it, Skip to the left and now we know. (Face center and clap four times.) Pop goes the weasel!"
16	**2. Walk CCW/Clap** Take 12 walking steps CCW. "Walk to the right and here we go And that's the way to do it, Walk to the right and now we know. (Face center and clap four times.) Pop goes the weasel!"

16

3. Stretch Arms Up-Down/Clap

Stretch arms up and down (12 cts).

"Stretch your arms up and down
And that's the way to do it,
Stretch your arms up and down.
(Face center and clap four times.)
Pop goes the weasell!"

16

4. Head-Shoulders-Hips/Clap

Repeat touching head, shoulders, hips, and clap
   (12 cts).

"Head-shoulders-hips and clap
And that's the way to do it,
Head-shoulders-hips and clap.
(Face center and clap four times.)
Pop goes the weasell!"

VARIATIONS AND SUGGESTIONS

Movement Options

"Slide to the L and here we go . . ."
"Gallop away and here we go. . ."
"Horses trot and keep the time. . ."
"Tiptoe L and don't be slow. . ."

In place of clapping, jump apart-together twice on the last line.

BLEKING

SWEDEN

BACKGROUND

The Bleking is synonymous with traditional folk dancing. The catchy, two-three pattern has counterparts in modern-day rhythms. This basic dance has the enduring quality of a true folk dance. For a definition of the basic step pattern of bleking, see page 225.

MUSIC (2/4)

"Bleking," 1188, Folkraft.

FORMATION

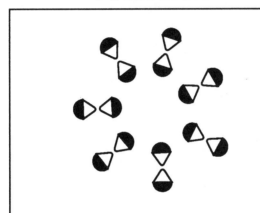

Pairs in double circle facing each other
(inside partner's back to center) with
both hands joined.

COUNTS	STEPS
Chord	Introduction (wait in place)
16	**1. Bleking**

1. Bleking
For a definition of bleking, see page 225.
Hop on L, extending R heel forward and thrusting R arm forward (1 ct). Hop onto R, extending L heel forward and thrusting L arm forward (1 ct). Extend feet in rapid succession as RLR, while thrusting alternate arms forward (2 cts).
Repeat beginning, hopping on R and extending L heel forward (L-R, LRL) 4 cts.
Repeat (R-L, RLR and L-R, LRL) 8 cts.

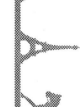

2. Step-Hops

For a definition of the step-hop, see page 226.

With arms extended sideways, take eight step-hops in place (inside partner begins on L, outside partner on R) while leaning to L and R alternately (8 cts).

Take seven step-hops, making a CW turn, and end with a stamp (8 cts).

VARIATIONS AND SUGGESTIONS

Step 1

It is easier for younger students to place hands on hips, or let the hands hang at sides.

Step 2

Do the eight step-hops with hands on own hips or at sides. Then dance four step-hops backward and four step-hops forward. As a mixer, veer L in the forward step-hops to find a new partner.

SHOES-A-DANCING

BELGIUM

BACKGROUND

In some rural areas of Belgium, wooden clogs are still worn to keep feet dry in wet farming country. Clogs are waterproof and warm.

Shoes-a-Dancing is based on the dance "Daar Liep Een Oude Vrouw." Its folk quality makes it a dance all ages can enjoy.

MUSIC (4/4)

"Dutch Wooden Shoes," Learning by Doing, Dancing, and Discovering 76, Educational Activities.

FORMATION

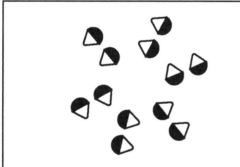

Pairs in double circle facing CCW, with inside hands joined and outside hands on hips.

COUNTS	STEPS
16	Introduction (wait in place)
16	**1. Running Steps Forward/Stamps** Moving CCW, take 12 running steps forward (inside partner begins on L, outside partner on R). Facing partner, join hands and stamp three times and hold (4 cts).
16	**2. Swing** For a definition of the swing, see page 227. Partners hook R elbows and swing CW, turning in place with 12 running steps. End facing CCW with three stamps, holding inside hands (4 cts).
32	**3. Running Steps Forward/Stamps/Swing** Repeat Steps 1 and 2, but partners end facing on the final stamps.

4. Away-Together/Stamps

Moving backward, inside partner steps LRL hold (4 cts).
Moving forward, same partner steps RLR hold (4 cts).
Same partner stamps in place LRLRLRL hold (8 cts).
(Outside partner does same steps on opposite foot.)
Repeat Step 4 (16 cts).

VARIATIONS AND SUGGESTIONS

Mixer

Each dancer veers L to a new partner on the last three stamps.

CSHEBOGAR

HUNGARY

BACKGROUND

In Hungarian, Cshebogar means "the beetle." Hungarian music, possibly of Gypsy origin, is known for its half-happy, half-sad tunes.

Cshebogar (CHAY-bo-gar), with its unique Hungarian spirit and dash, has had a long tenure as a school dance. The slow two-step is reminiscent of the national dance, the Csardas, and the typical cross step (Bokazo) brings the dance to an end. For the definitions of the two-step and bokazo, see pages 225 and 226.

MUSIC (2/4)

"Cshebogar," World of Fun Series M 101, World of Fun (see Ed Kremers' Folk Showplace).

FORMATION

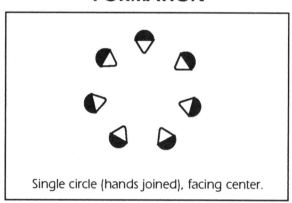

Single circle (hands joined), facing center.

COUNTS	STEPS
Chord	Introduction (wait in place)
16	**1. Sliding R and L** Moving CW, take seven slides beginning on L and end touching R beside L (8 cts). Moving CCW, take seven slides beginning on R and end touching L beside R (8 cts).
16	**2. Center and Back** Walk toward center with a LRL and stamp R beside L (no weight on R) 4 cts. Walk backward from center with a RLR and stamp L beside R (no weight on L) 4 cts. Repeat (8 cts).

8

3. Csardas (Slow Two-Step)

For a definition of the two-step, see page 226.

(The music slows to indicate this step.)

Step sideways on L, close R to L, step sideways on L, close
R to L (no weight on R) 4 cts.

Step sideways on R, close L to R, step sideways on R,
close L to R (no weight on L) 4 cts.

There is a slight knee bend on each close.

4

4. Step-Stamp

Step sideways on L and stamp R beside L, flexing knees
(2 cts).

Step sideways on R and stamp L beside R, flexing knees
(2 cts).

4

5. Bokazo

For a definition of the bokazo, see page 225.

Hop on L and touch R toe in front, hop on L and touch R
toe sideways opposite L, jump bringing feet together,
and hold (4 cts).

16

6. Csardas/Step-Stamp/Bokazo

Repeat Steps 3-5.

VARIATIONS AND SUGGESTIONS

Formation

Hands should be joined shoulder high, elbows bent so arms form a "W."

TROIKA
RUSSIA

BACKGROUND

The Russian troika is a fast-moving circle dance in which dancers are grouped into threes. Each trio symbolizes the three horses that gallop abreast as they pull a Russian sleigh across the snow.

Troika (TROY-kuh) denotes a Russian vehicle drawn by a team of three horses abreast. This basic and unsophisticated dance has long been a familiar one with traditional folk dancers. The zest of Russian music and dance provides an opportunity for fun and exercise.

MUSIC (4/4)

"Troika," 1170, Folkraft, or "Troika," MH 1059, Folk Dancer (see Ed Kremers' Folk Showplace or Folkraft).

FORMATION

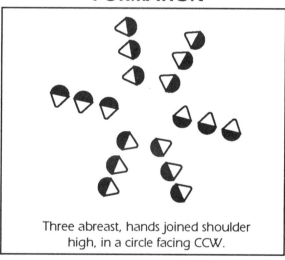

Three abreast, hands joined shoulder high, in a circle facing CCW.

COUNTS	STEPS
8	Introduction (wait in place)
16	**1. Run Forward** Moving diagonally R, take four running steps beginning on R. Moving diagonally L, take four running steps beginning on L. Moving CCW, take eight running steps directly forward.

16

2. Run Through the Arches

Center dancer and L-hand partner raise joined
hands in an arch. R-hand dancer runs eight steps
through arch as center dancer follows.
Center dancer and R-hand partner form an arch and
L-hand dancer runs eight steps through arch as
center dancer follows.

32

3. Trios Circle and Stamp

Joining hands, the trio circles with 12 running steps L,
ending with three stamps.
Repeat circling R and end with three stamps.
Release hands and end facing CCW three abreast.

VARIATIONS AND SUGGESTIONS

Step 1

May simply take 16 running steps forward.

Step 3

Mature dancers may substitute a 12-ct grapevine for circling with
running steps. For a definition of a grapevine, see page 227.

Mixer

In place of the last three stamps, the center dancer may pop under the
arch of the other two and move forward CCW to a new trio.

ATLANTIC MIXER

GERMANY

BACKGROUND

After World War II, the United States, as well as other countries, got together to help rebuild Europe, including Germany.

This recreational dance was introduced in Germany in 1948. The style of this German dance was probably influenced by the presence of American troops and American square dancers in Germany. Its style contrasts with some of the older, traditional German dances.

MUSIC (2/4)

"Atlantic Mixer," SP 23 050, Tanz Records (see Ed Kremers' Folk Showplace).

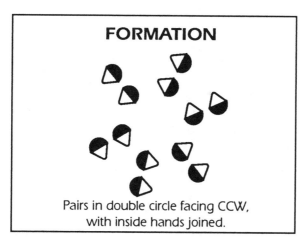

FORMATION

Pairs in double circle facing CCW, with inside hands joined.

COUNTS	STEPS
8	Introduction (wait in place)
32	**1. Promenade** For a definition of the promenade, see page 226. Facing CCW, partners promenade (walk) forward with 16 steps (inside partner begins on L, outside partner on R). Outside partner makes 1/2 turn and walks 16 steps in reverse direction (CW) as inside partner continues with 16 steps forward (CCW).
16	**2. Star R and L** For a definition of the star R or L, see page 226. Inside partner grasps the nearest partner of a pair and they star R (R hands held high and clasped with forearms touching) 8 cts and then star L (8 cts).

3. Swing Partner

For definitions of the Swing and "Buzz" step, see pages 225 and 227.

Partners swing with skipping or "Buzz" steps.

VARIATIONS AND SUGGESTIONS

Step 2

Star R only and then do a do-sa-do (partners pass R shoulders, back to back, and pass L shoulders making a circle pattern around each other) 8 cts. For a definition of the do-sa-do, see page 226.

Music

This dance may be done to most American square dance tunes. The 64 counts will coincide well with square dance music.

SAVILA SE BELA LOZA

YUGOSLAVIA

BACKGROUND

Savila Se Bela Loza (sah-VEE-lah seh BEH-la LOH-zah), translated "a grapevine entwined in itself," is an easy, yet energetic Serbian dance. In folk dance, it is classified as a "Kolo" (dance performed in a line or broken circle). At the time this book went to press, Yugoslavia was in a state of flux. Yugoslavia will soon be divided into separate republics or countries, each with its own borders and government.

MUSIC (2/4)

"Savila Se Bela Loza," Dances Around the World 572, Educational Activities, or "Savila Se Bela Loza," 1496, Folkraft.

FORMATION

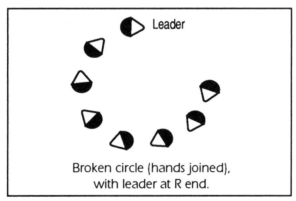

Leader

Broken circle (hands joined),
with leader at R end.

COUNTS	STEPS
8	Introduction (wait in place)
40	**1. Running/Stamps** Moving CCW, take16 running steps. (Feet should be close to floor and under the body.) Facing center, stamp three times, RLR and hold (4 cts). Moving CW, take 16 running steps in reverse direction. Facing center, stamp three times, LRL and hold (4 cts).
24	**2. Schottische Steps Forward** For a definition of schottische, see page 226. Moving slightly sideways R, step R-close-R-hop (4 cts). Moving sideways L, step L-close-L-hop (4 cts). Repeat schottische to the R and L twice (16 cts).

VARIATIONS AND SUGGESTIONS

Step 1

More mature dancers may take 18 running steps CCW ending with a step-hop R. Repeat the same in reverse direction, CW. The leader may "snake" or wind the line, adding to the challenge. (For a definition of the step-hop, see page 226.)

TROPANKA
BULGARIA

BACKGROUND

Tropanka (tro-PON-kah) is also known as the "Bulgarian Stamping Dance." It is one of the earliest Bulgarian dances enjoyed in our nation. Though many more challenging versions exist, this choreography is easy and fun.

MUSIC (2/4)

"Tropanka," Honor Your Partner International Folk Dance Series 22, Educational Activities.

FORMATION

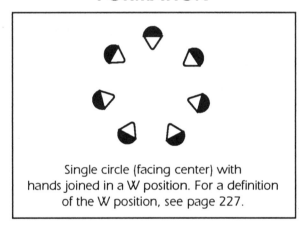

Single circle (facing center) with hands joined in a W position. For a definition of the W position, see page 227.

COUNTS	STEPS
16	Introduction (wait in place)
32	**1. Run and Stamp**
	Moving CCW, take five running steps beginning on R, face center and stamp L beside R twice (8 cts).
	Moving CW, take five running steps beginning on L, face center and stamp R beside L twice (8 cts).
	Repeat runs and stamps CCW and CW (16 cts).
32	**2. Step-Hop, Swing/Stamp**
	For a definition of the step-hop, see page 226.
	Step-hop on R while swinging L in front of R (2 cts).

Step-hop on L while swinging R in front of L
(2 cts).
Step on R and stamp L beside R twice (4 cts).
Step-hop on L while swinging R in front of L (2 cts).
Step-hop on R while swinging L in front of R (2 cts).
Step on L and stamp R beside L twice (4 cts).
Repeat step-hops RL, stamps, step-hops LR, stamps (16 cts.)

32

3. Step-Hop/Stamp

Moving toward center, step-hop on R (2 cts) and on L
(2 cts). Step forward on R and stamp L beside R twice
(4 cts). Gradually raise joined hands upward while
moving forward and stamping.
Moving backward, step-hop on L (2 cts) and on R (2 cts).
Step backward on L and stamp R beside L twice (4 cts).
Gradually lower joined hands while moving backward
and stamping.
Repeat Step 3 (16 cts).

VARIATIONS AND SUGGESTIONS

Hand Placement

While learning the dance, it is easier for elementary students to drop
hands on Steps 2 and 3 and place hands on hips.

ČEREŠNIČKY

CZECHOSLOVAKIA

BACKGROUND

Čerešničky (CHAIR-esh-neech-kee) is a circle dance from Moravia. Because of the simplicity of this dance and its inviting music, it is a popular item on folk dance programs throughout the country. At the time this book went to press, Czechoslovakia was in a state of flux. The country will probably be divided into two countries, each with its own borders and government.

MUSIC (2/4)

"Čerešničky," WT-MBH 1003 EP, Worldtone (see Folkraft).

FORMATION

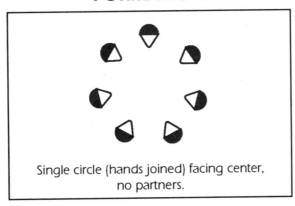

Single circle (hands joined) facing center,
no partners.

COUNTS	STEPS
32	**1. Step Sideways/Step and Close** Moving CW, step sideways on L, close R to L (2 cts). Repeat (2 cts). Step sideways on L (2 cts) and close R to L (2 cts). Cue the steps by saying, "Step-close, step-close, step and close." Repeat all step-closes moving sideways R (8 cts). Repeat Step 1 (16 cts).
32	**2. Chorus** <u>Cross Step</u> For a definition of the cross step, see page 225. Moving CW, step on R across L, step sideways on L, step on R across L, and step sideways on L (4 cts). <u>Key Step</u> Stamp R in front of L, step sideways on L, bring R to L with a click, and hold (4 cts). Cue the step by saying "Cross-side-together-hold."

Grapevine
For a definition of the grapevine, see page 227.
Moving CW, step on R across L, step sideways on
L, step on R behind L, step sideways on L (4 cts).
Key Step
Repeat Key Step (4 cts).
Moving CW, repeat all of Step 2 (16 cts).

VARIATIONS AND SUGGESTIONS

Step 2

For elementary students, do a 12-ct grapevine ending with the key step. Repeat twice.

Primary

Step 1: Same

Step 2: Moving toward center, clap own hands while walking forward LRLR (4 cts). Then, moving away from center, walk backward LRLR (4 cts).

Moving CW, join hands and take eight skips (may walk or slide).
Repeat Step 2 (16 cts).

KALVELIS

LITHUANIA

BACKGROUND

Kalvelis represents one of a number of enjoyable Lithuanian dances. Also known as "The Little Blacksmith," this mixer's refrain denotes a blacksmith hammering on an anvil. This "work" dance is similar to the Japanese "work" dance Tanko Bushi.

MUSIC (2/4)

"Kalvelis," 1418, Folkraft.

FORMATION

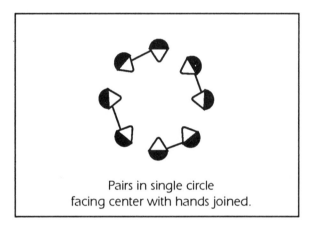

Pairs in single circle
facing center with hands joined.

COUNTS	STEPS
4	Introduction (wait in place)
32	**1. Circle R and L with Running Polka Steps** For a definition of the running polka, see page 226. Moving CCW, circle with seven running polka steps RLR, LRL, and so on (14 cts). The polka is a running two-step (step-close-step) 2 cts. End facing center with three quick stamps (2 cts). Moving CW, circle with seven polka steps (14 cts). End facing partner with three quick stamps (2 cts).
32	**2. Chorus: Hammer the Anvil** With partners facing, clap own hands four times (L on R, R on L, L on R, and R on L) 4 cts. Partners hook R elbows and turn in four skips (4 cts).

Repeat clapping and turning three more times (24 cts).
End facing center.

32

3. Center and Back

Moving toward center, partner on the left takes three polka steps forward and does three stamps while turning to face partner (8 cts).

Moving forward, same partner takes three polka steps back to place and does three stamps while turning to face center (8 cts).

Partner on right now repeats same steps as the other partner did (16 cts).

On last three stamps partners face.

32

4. Chorus: Hammer the Anvil

Repeat Step 2.

32

5. Grand R and L with Running Polka Steps

For a definition of the grand R and L, see page 226.

Partners face and grasp R hands to pull by and extend L hand to next dancer. Pull by with L hand to extend R hand to next dancer. Continue moving around circle extending alternate hands. One set of partners will be moving CW and the other will be moving CCW with 16 polka steps. Meet a new partner on the last 2 cts.

32

6. Chorus: Hammer the Anvil

Repeat Step 2.

VARIATIONS AND SUGGESTIONS

Step 1

Younger dancers can walk, skip, or slide instead of doing polka steps.

Step 2

Take four stamps in place rather than hooking elbows and swinging.

Formation

Dancers who cannot find a new partner go to the center, find a partner, and then rejoin the circle.

KOROBUSHKA
RUSSIA

BACKGROUND

Korobushka (kuh-ROW-bush-kuh) is also known as "The Peddler's Pack" or "Little Basket." This version is danced in a line without partners. Its simplicity offers a more helpful introduction to the dance for beginning dancers.

MUSIC (4/4)

"Korobushka," Dances Around the World 572, Educational Activities.

FORMATION

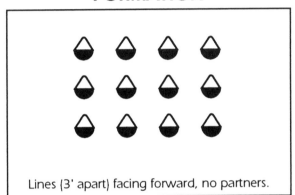

Lines (3' apart) facing forward, no partners.

COUNTS	STEPS
8	Introduction (wait in place)

12	**1. Schottische Forward-Backward** For a definition of the schottische, see page 226. Moving forward, step L-R-L-hop (4 cts). Moving backward, step R-L-R-hop (4 cts). Moving forward, step L-R-L-hop (4 cts).
4	**2. Hungarian Break (Bokazo)** For a definition of the bokazo, see page 225. Hop on L and touch R toe in front of L, hop on L and touch R toe sideways opposite L, jump bringing feet together, and hold.
4	**3. Three-Step Turn** For a definition of the three-step turn, see page 226. Moving CW in place, make a complete turn stepping RLR. Touch L beside R and clap hands once.

4   **4. Two-Step**
For a definition of the two-step, see page 226.
Moving L, step sideways on L, close R to L, step sideways
on L and touch R to L, clapping hands once.

4   **5. Stamps**
Stamp R forward strongly and then step on R beside L
(2 cts).
Stamp L forward strongly and step on L beside R (2 cts).

4   **6. Hungarian Break**
Repeat Step 2.

16   **7. Three-Step Turn/Two-Step/Stamps/Hungarian Break**
Repeat Steps 3-6.

VARIATIONS AND SUGGESTIONS

Formation
The dance may be done in a single circle facing center.

NEVER ON SUNDAY

GREECE

BACKGROUND

Throughout Greece, local festivals and celebrations are alive with folk dances. Folk music is performed with clarinets and stringed instruments called "bouzoukis." Festivals celebrating ancient Greek dramas are performed in round outdoor theaters built about the time of Christ.

This version of Never on Sunday adds a step often seen in the taverna dance, "Slow Hasapiko." The dance provides enough of a challenge to make it both unique and recreational.

MUSIC (4/4)

"Never on Sunday," Dances Around the World 572, Educational Activities.

FORMATION

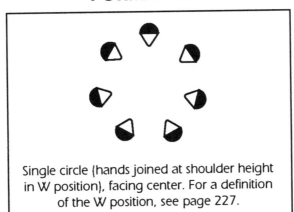

Single circle (hands joined at shoulder height in W position), facing center. For a definition of the W position, see page 227.

COUNTS	STEPS
28	Introduction (wait in place)
4	**1. Step and Point** Step on R in place, hold, point L toe in front of R, hold.
4	**2. Grapevine** For a definition of the grapevine, see page 227. Moving CCW, step on L in back of R, step sideways on R, step on L across R, bring R by L ankle facing center (4 cts).

8

3. Two-Step (The "Pie")
For a definition of the two-step, see page 226.
Moving forward diagonally, step towards L with a
two-step RLR, pivot slightly R.
Moving backward diagonally, with a two-step LRL.
(The two-step is angled and pie-shaped.)

16

4. Step and Point/Gravevine/Two-Step
Repeat Steps 1-3.

32

5. Taverna Cross Steps
For a definition of the cross step, see page 225.
Moving sideways L (CW), step on R across L. Moving
slightly L, step back on L. Again cross R over L, and
step backward on L. A third time cross R over L, but
swing L by R ankle (6 cts). Cue the step by saying
"R and R and R and."
Moving sideways R (CCW), repeat same action of
"threes" in the opposite direction with a LR, LR, LR,
and swing R by L ankle (6 cts).
Repeat the same action but do "twos" (CW), RL, RL and
(CCW) LR, LR (8 cts).
Repeat the same action but do "ones," RL, LR (4 cts).
Step sideways R (2 cts) and draw L to R (2 cts).
Step sideways L (2 cts) and draw R to L (2 cts).
Cue the step by saying, "Step and draw, step and draw."

VARIATIONS AND SUGGESTIONS

Formation
May be danced in short lines.

NIXIE DANCE
DENMARK

BACKGROUND

The original Nixie Dance tells of the Nixie (water spirit) who appears at different times of the year. This is a revised version of the dance.

MUSIC (3/4)

"Nixie Dance," Dances Around the World 572, Educational Activities.

FORMATION

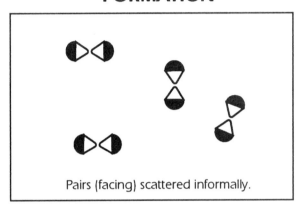

Pairs (facing) scattered informally.

COUNTS	STEPS
12	Introduction (wait in place)
12	**1. Leap and Extend Foot** Leap in place on to L and extend R heel forward, toe up (3 cts). Leap in place on to R and extend L heel forward, toe up (3 cts). Repeat both leaps (6 cts).
24	**2. Jump Apart-Together** Jump in place landing with feet apart (1 ct). Jump landing with feet together bouncing twice (2 cts). Repeat jump series six more times (18 cts). End with two stamps RL (2 cts).
12	**3. Leap and Extend Foot** Repeat Step 1.

4. Clap/Running Waltz/Stamps

For a definition of the running waltz, see page 226.

While clapping hands, each dancer makes a 1/2 turn L and takes seven running waltz steps (LRL, RLR, and so on), moving freely to end with two stamps RL. Meet another partner or end in a small group facing each other.

VARIATIONS AND SUGGESTIONS

Step 4

Encourage dancers to find a new partner of the opposite sex. However, accept children's freedom of choice. Students may also dance in groups of three or four.

Hand Placement

In Danish dances, free hands are often placed on the hips.

Creative Movement

Use the same pattern with other kinds of music, such as Latin, square dance, or rock. Invite students to create new dances.

EINS ZWEI DREI

GERMANY

BACKGROUND

"Eins Zwei Drei" (ine-ts zvi dry) is a children's dance based on a German square dance from Holstein.

MUSIC (2/4)

"Eins Zwei Drei," 1522, Folkraft.

FORMATION

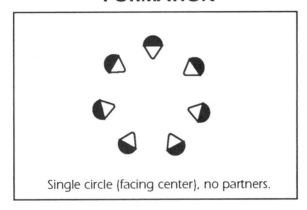

Single circle (facing center), no partners.

COUNTS	STEPS
8	Introduction (wait in place)
32	**1. Walk Forward-Backward/Slide**

1. Walk Forward-Backward/Slide

Moving forward, step on L, step on R, close L to R and hold (4 cts) while clapping hands vertically like cymbals three times.

Moving backward, step on R, step on L, close R to L and hold (4 cts) while clapping hands vertically like cymbals three times.

Turn so L shoulder faces center and take three slides toward center and touch R beside L (4 cts).

Retrace steps by taking three slides away from center and touch L beside R (4 cts). End facing center.

Repeat walks forward-backward and slides (16 cts).

2. Heel Placing/Slide

Place L heel forward and step on L beside R
(2 cts).
Place R heel forward and step on R beside L
(2 cts).
Place L heel forward and step on L beside R
(2 cts).
Join hands shoulder high (2 cts).
Moving CW, take eight slides (8 cts).
Repeat heel placing, starting with R, then L, then
R (6 cts).
Join hands shoulder high (2 cts).
Moving CCW, take eight slides (8 cts).

VARIATIONS AND SUGGESTIONS

Step 1

In place of sliding toward and away from center, jump with feet apart and then together for 8 cts.

Partner Dance

Pairs in a single circle facing center (outside partner on inside partner's R).

Step 1: Walking forward-backward is the same. Pairs face each other and join hands to slide toward and away from center.

Step 2: Pairs continue to face each other for the heel placing. Then dancers face center to join hands before sliding CW or CCW.

RIJPE GERST

HOLLAND

BACKGROUND

Holland is well-known throughout the world for its beautiful tulips. Every year in the spring, millions of tulips are grown and harvested for their bulbs and flowers.

Rijpe Gerst (RAY-per GUR-stuh) is an excellent children's dance. This harvest dance may be performed with a partner or as a mixer.

MUSIC (4/4)

"Rijpe Gerst," 1522, Folkraft.

FORMATION

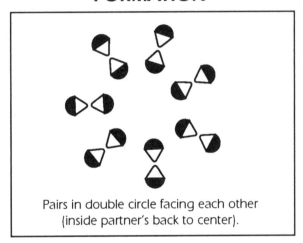

Pairs in double circle facing each other
(inside partner's back to center).

COUNTS	STEPS
8	Introduction (wait in place)
8	**1. Clap** Clap both hands with partner and clap own hands (2 cts). Clap R with partner and clap own hands (2 cts). Clap L with partner and clap own hands (2 cts). Clap both hands with partner and clap own hands (2 cts).
8	**2. Mow Barley** Bending from the waist, strike R hand with L and then L with R alternately at waist level, imitating mowing the barley. Hands hit each other at the center of body.

16   **3. Clap/Mow Barley**

Repeat Steps 1 and 2.

8   **4. Step and Close**

Moving sideways L, inside partner steps on L and closes R to L. In place, same partner stamps LRL (4 cts). At the same time, outside partner moves sideways R, stepping on R and closing L to R. In place, same partner stamps RLR.

Inside partner repeats steps moving sideways R and at the same time outside partner moves sideways L (4 cts).

16   **5. Swing or R Star**

For a definition of these steps, see pages 226 and 227.

Partners hook R elbows and turn in place making two turns with 12 small running steps.

Drop elbows, stamp three times, and hold.

32   **6. Step and Close/Swing**

Repeat Steps 4 and 5, but swing only once around in Step 5 (16 cts).

Inside partner then moves forward on the inside to meet a new partner. Outside partner advances in the reverse direction on the outside to meet a new partner. This partner switch takes 12 cts of running steps plus three stamps (16 cts).

VARIATIONS AND SUGGESTIONS

Step 2

To simplify the mowing, join hands and swing them sideways. Or, extend hands forward and backward.

Step 4

Move sideways with a step-close-step-hold.

Step 5

For R star position, partners hold up joined R hands with elbows bent and forearms adjacent.

SHOEMAKER'S DANCE
DENMARK

BACKGROUND

This folk dance "giant" is welcomed by teachers and students. It is an example of a "work" dance that depicts shoemaking. Other such "work" dances might depict farming or fishing.

MUSIC (2/4)

"Shoemaker's Dance," Rhythmic Stick Activities 55, Educational Activities.

FORMATION

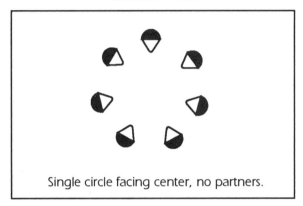

Single circle facing center, no partners.

<u>COUNTS</u>   <u>STEPS</u>

Chord   Introduction (wait in place)

16   **1. Chorus: Wind-Pull-Clap/Tap**
        Bending elbows, hold arms chest high horizontally with fists clenched. Wind thread by rolling one arm over the other and hold (2 cts). Reverse roll and hold (2 cts).
        Break thread by pulling arms apart, jerking elbows outward twice (2 cts).
        Tap pegs by clapping own hands three times (2 cts).
        Repeat winding forward and reverse (4 cts).
        Repeat breaking thread (2 cts).
        Drive pegs by tapping one fist on the other three times (2 cts).

8   **2. Running Steps**
Moving CW, take seven running steps and hold (4 cts).
Moving CCW, take seven running steps and hold (4 cts).

8   **3. Heel Placing**
Extend L heel forward and then step on L beside R (2 cts).
Extend R heel forward and step on R beside L (2 cts).
Repeat L and R heels (4 cts).

VARIATIONS AND SUGGESTIONS

Step 3

More mature students may run forward seven steps and hold and backward seven steps and hold.

Partner Dance

Partners in double circle facing each other (inside partner's back to
center).
Step 1: Same
Step 2: Run backward seven steps and advance seven steps to a new
partner.
Step 3: Do heel placing with new partner.

Shoemaker's Stick Game

Give each student a rhythm stick to hold in each hand. (Sticks may be
plastic, wooden, or newspaper rolled and bound with masking tape.
Remind children to be careful when handling sticks.)
Step 1: Roll sticks forward and reverse (4 cts).
Pull elbows outward (2 cts).
Tap one stick on the other three times (2 cts).
Holding sticks in front of chest, alternate striking R on L and L on R
(8 cts).
Steps 2 and 3: Invite students to create their own movements. Vary the
time, force, and space used.

Mixer

Partners in double circle facing CCW (inside partner's back to center).
Step 1: Same
Step 2: Inside partner faces slightly forward L and does a toe-heel with the
L foot (2 cts) and takes three steps diagonally forward LRL (2 cts). Same
partner now turns to face slightly R and does a toe-heel with the R foot
(2 cts) and takes three steps diagonally forward RLR (2 cts). Outside
partner does the same steps but begins facing slightly R and then
faces L.
This creates a diamond pattern when both partners move away from
and then toward each other. For the last 8 cts, inside partners may
advance to new partners.

MIDDLE EAST
GAMES AND DANCES

GOOSH VA DAMAGH (EAR AND NOSE)

IRAN

TYPE

Quiet classroom game

SOMETHING ABOUT THE COUNTRY

Life in Iran is guided by the Muslim religion. Tradition is important to Iranians. Iranian women dress in modest garments that include a "chador." The chador is a long, wraparound cloth that covers the head and is sometimes used as a veil to cover the face.

EQUIPMENT

None

FORMATION

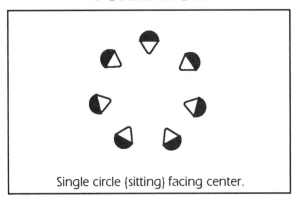

Single circle (sitting) facing center.

DESCRIPTION

Choose one player to be the chief. The chief directs the play. Before the game starts, players together repeat this nonsense rhyme:

Ala hop, sang torop?
Peshgel boz, khoda biamorz, hop!

Players try not to laugh, smile, or make any loud cries while reciting the rhyme or playing the game. The chief lightly taps the ear, nose, or hair of the player on his or her L. This player passes on the same action to the player on his or her L. The action passes around the circle until it reaches the chief again. The chief then starts another action around the circle, such as tickling the next player or making a funny face. Any player who laughs, giggles, or makes any noise has to leave the game or pay a forfeit (see page 9). The winner is the player who shows the most self-control by not smiling, laughing, or making a sound.

PEBBLE TOSS

LEBANON

TYPE
Quiet classroom game

SOMETHING ABOUT THE COUNTRY

Lebanon does not have laws requiring children to pursue an education. Even so, most children do attend elementary and secondary school. Many of the children go to public schools, but more than half attend private schools which charge tuition.

EQUIPMENT
✓Buttons
✓Cans or cartons (one per player)

FORMATION

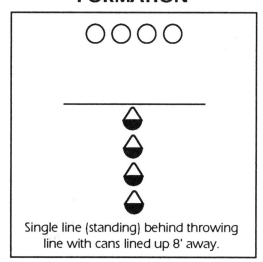

Single line (standing) behind throwing
line with cans lined up 8' away.

DESCRIPTION

Place cans (one per player) close together in a straight line in front of each group. Each player has an equal number of buttons (3-4). Each player in turn stands at the throwing line and tosses the buttons, one by one, into his or her can. The winner is the player with the most buttons in his or her can, whether that player or someone else tossed them in.

BLI YADAYIM (WITHOUT HANDS)

ISRAEL

TYPE
Active playground game

SOMETHING ABOUT THE COUNTRY
Hebrew and Arabic are the two official languages of Israel. Both languages appear on Israeli money and stamps. Many Israeli children are bilingual.

EQUIPMENT
✓Jump rope (one per group)
✓Paper hats (one per player)

FORMATION

Single line of 4-5 players (standing), holding a jump rope in front of them with hats placed a few feet in front.

DESCRIPTION
Place one paper hat per player a few feet from group members. Each member of the group holds the jump rope with both hands. On a given signal, each group, still holding the rope, runs toward the hats. Players try to get a paper hat on their heads without using their hands. If a player uses his or her hands or drops the rope, the whole group is disqualified. Players can help each other using their heads, teeth, and feet. The group that returns first with each member wearing a hat is the winner.

KUKLA

TURKEY

TYPE
Active playground game

SOMETHING ABOUT THE COUNTRY

Turkish rugs, known for their beauty and detailed weavings, are popular items in the United States. Not only are they beautiful, but many of the rugs have special meanings, too. A jagged border, for example, may mean luck for a marriage, red sometimes signifies courage, and white represents a pure heart.

EQUIPMENT
✓Can or milk carton
✓Beanbags (one per player)

FORMATION:

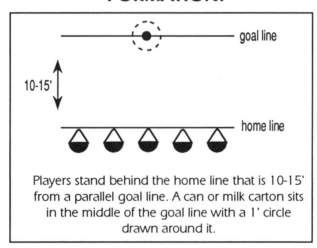

Players stand behind the home line that is 10-15' from a parallel goal line. A can or milk carton sits in the middle of the goal line with a 1' circle drawn around it.

DESCRIPTION

Select one player as the guard to stand behind the goal line. Players behind the home line toss their beanbags one at a time toward the can. The object is to knock the can over and, if possible, out of the circle drawn around it. Once the can is knocked over, the players run quickly to retrieve their beanbags. The guard grabs the can and sets it back up inside the circle and then tries to tag one of the players retrieving a beanbag. Players whose beanbags land in front of the goal line must retrieve their beanbags and try to return safely back to the home line.

Players whose beanbags land behind the goal line have a choice—they may try to grab their beanbag and return to the home line or they may stand in safety on their beanbag in which case the guard cannot tag them. Players who choose to stand on their beanbag must remain there until another player knocks over the can. Then they can pick up their beanbag and return to the home line. If the guard can tag a player before he or she crosses back over the home line with the beanbag, the tagged player becomes the new guard. The game is over when every player but one has been the guard. That player is the winner.

MAGURA (PECAN HOLE)

IRAQ

TYPE
Quiet classroom game

SOMETHING ABOUT THE COUNTRY
Oil is the primary source of income in Iraq. In fact, 90% of Iraq's income is based on this natural resource. Money generated from oil pays for modern improvements, such as clean water and electricity throughout Iraq, as well as for improvements in education.

EQUIPMENT
✓Pecans (ten per player)
✓Milk cartons
✓Wooden backstops

FORMATION

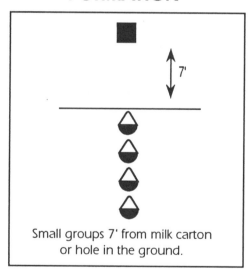

Small groups 7' from milk carton
or hole in the ground.

DESCRIPTION
Place a milk carton about 7' from each team, or dig a small hole in the ground 4" in diameter and 3" deep. Place a small wooden backstop behind the hole or carton. Choose one player in each group to be the "owner" of the hole or carton. The first player on each team throws all of his or her

pecans at once toward the hole or carton. If an even number of pecans fall into the hole or carton, the owner gives these pecans back to the thrower and keeps the ones that did not go in. If an odd number of pecans go into the hole or carton, the owner keeps these and gives back to the thrower the ones that did not go in. The next player then takes a turn. The owner may "sell" the hole or carton at any time to one of the other players and become a thrower. The game ends when one player loses all of his or her pecans. The winner is the player with the highest number of pecans.

AROUND WE GO

ISRAEL

BACKGROUND

Some Israelis live and work in collective communities called "kibbutzim," where farmers share all property and combine their labor.

Around We Go, also known as "Uga, Uga Uga (Ooga, Ooga, Ooga)," is a lively children's dance or game. "Uga" in Hebrew means "circle," but also may mean "cake." Perhaps performing this happy dance is as pleasurable as eating cake.

MUSIC (2/4)

"Around We Go," Learning by Doing, Dancing, and Discovering 76, Educational Activities.

FORMATION

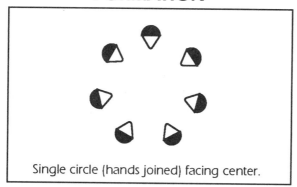

Single circle (hands joined) facing center.

COUNTS   STEPS

8   Introduction (wait in place)

16   **1. Circle L (CW) Walking**
Moving CW, take 16 walking steps beginning on L. End facing center and drop hands. (Use other basic movements, such as sliding, tiptoeing, or skipping, each time the dance repeats).

16   **2. Squat and Up**
Squat (2 cts) and get up (2 cts).
Repeat (4 cts).
Squat and hold (4 cts) and get up and hold (4 cts).

4   **3. Interlude**
Mark time in place RLRL before beginning dance again.

VARIATIONS AND SUGGESTIONS

Sing Along

Dancers can sing along as they dance.

Uga, uga, uga
Ba-ma-gal na-chu-ga
Nis-to-ve-va kol ha-yom
Ad a-sher nim-za ma-kom

La-she-vet la-kum
La-she-vet la-kum
La-she-vet, la-she-vet
La-she-vet kol ha-yom!

Around and around and around
Let's go in a circle.
We'll go round all the day,
'Til we find a place to stay.

To sit and get up,
To sit and get up,
To sit, to sit
To sit all day!

Advanced

Step 1: Grapevine CW. For a definition of the grapevine, see page 227. Moving CW, step R over L, step sideways L, step R in back of L, step sideways on L (4 cts). Move joined hands in and out at waist level with the grapevine. Repeat grapevine three more times moving L. End dropping hands.

Step 2: Get Down. For a definition of the get-down step, see page 227. Step forward on R toward center bending R knee, step in place on L, step R and L in place while clapping two times (4 cts). Repeat three more times. Mark time in place RLRL for interlude before beginning dance again.

TZADIK KATAMAR YIFRACH

ISRAEL

BACKGROUND

An independent nation since 1948, Israel is the homeland for Jews from all over the world and for many Arabs as well. Jerusalem, the holy city for Jews, Muslims, and Christians, is the capital of Israel.

Among the legions of Israeli dances, Tzadik Katamar Yifrach (sah-DEEK kah-tah-MAR yee-FROCK) stands out for its eloquence and simplicity. This adaptation for young children flows pleasantly and smoothly.

MUSIC (4/4)

"Tzadik Katamar," 10015, Worldtone (see Folkraft).

FORMATION

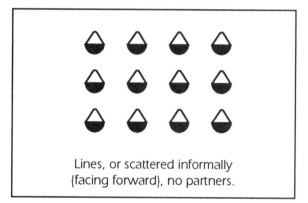

Lines, or scattered informally
(facing forward), no partners.

COUNTS	STEPS
16	Introduction (wait in place)
16	**1. Walk Forward-Clap/Walk Backward-Clap** Take four steps forward (4 cts), clap three times and hold (4 cts). Take four steps backward (4 cts), clap three times and hold (4 cts).
8	**2. Stretch Arms** Turning torso slightly L, stretch arms upward in a "Y" shape (1 ct). Facing forward, bring hands to chest (1 ct). Turning torso slightly R, stretch arms upward in a "Y" shape (1 ct). Facing forward, bring hands to chest (1 ct). Repeat all (4 cts).

8   **3. Slap and Clap**
Bend forward and slap thighs twice (2 cts).
Straighten and clap once and hold (2 cts).
Repeat all (4 cts).

16   **4. Stretch Arms/Slap and Clap**
Repeat Steps 2 and 3.

VARIATIONS AND SUGGESTIONS

Step 1

Take walking steps in place.

Step 2

Stretch arms overhead and bring down to chest level, omitting turning torso.

Step 3

Lean sideways L and extend hands to clap twice. Straighten and clap once in front of chest and hold. Younger children can slap thighs for 7 cts and hold.

HALAY

ARMENIA

BACKGROUND

Armenians have a strong national identity, despite being absorbed by both the now disbanded Soviet Union and Turkey shortly after World War I. Armenians speak their own distinct language.

Though originally a line dance done primarily by men, this version of Halay (HAH-leh) has been adapted for all to enjoy.

MUSIC (4/4)

"Halay," 1530, Folkraft.

FORMATION

Single line of 5-7 dancers (side by side).

COUNTS	STEPS
8	Introduction (wait in place)
4	**1. Basic Line Step** Facing front (dancers' shoulders adjacent), step sideways on R, step on L behind R, step sideways on R, lift bent L knee toward R just off the floor.
4	**2. Chug-Jump** Dip both knees diagonally L and chug (slightly) forward on balls of both feet (1 ct). Chug backward, lifting heels and chugging a short step on balls of feet, straightening knees and facing front (1 ct). Repeat chugging forward and backward (2 cts).

VARIATIONS AND SUGGESTIONS

Step 1

Lean forward from the waist up and use a bouncy step.

Step 2

It might help to think of the chug as a twist-jump.

Formation

Adult groups hold bodies very close to each other when doing this dance. This is a dance performed in unison with togetherness and sharing.

MAYIM MAYIM

ISRAEL

BACKGROUND

Yearly averages of precipitation in Israel can vary from over 40 inches in the northern Galilean to one inch in the southern desert region. Winter is the rainy season in Israel, with summer being almost completely dry.

"Mayim Mayim" (MY-yim MY-yim) meaning "Water Water," reflects the importance of water in this vital, small country. The dance movements express the joy of finding water and the motion of waves as they break on the shores of Galilee. This joyous dance is an older Israeli dance carrying a strong folk quality, energy, and a feeling of togetherness.

MUSIC (2/4)

"Mayim Mayim," 1475, Folkraft.

FORMATION

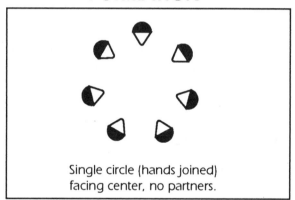

Single circle (hands joined)
facing center, no partners.

COUNTS	STEPS
8	Introduction (wait in place)
16	**1. Grapevine (Cherkessia Step)** For a definition of the grapevine, see page 227. Moving CW, step on R across L, step sideways on L, step on R in back of L, leap on to L, turning to face center bringing R near L ankle (4 cts). Moving CW, repeat grapevine three more times (12 cts).

16   **2. Running Forward and Back**

Moving toward center, take four running steps forward
(RLRL). Accent first step with a bend and gradually lift arms.
Moving away from center, take four running steps backward
(RLRL). Accent first step and gradually lower arms.
Repeat running steps forward and back (8 cts).

4   **3. Interlude: Running**

Facing CW, move forward with three running steps (RLR).
Facing center, touch L beside R (no weight on L).

8   **4. Hop**

Hop on R and touch or tap L in front of R (1 ct).
Hop on R and touch L sideways opposite R (1 ct).
Repeat hops three more times (6 cts). End with weight on L.

8   **5. Tap**

Drop hands. With weight on L, tap R toe in front of L while
clapping hands in front at chest level (1 ct).
Hop on L and tap R toe to the side while extending arms
sideways shoulder high (1 ct).
Repeat toe taps and arm action three more times (6 cts).

VARIATIONS AND SUGGESTIONS

Primary

Step 1: Walk CCW and CW.

Moving CCW, take seven walking steps beginning on R. End
touching L to R and facing CW.
Moving CW, take seven walking steps beginning on L. End touching
R to L.

Step 2: Forward and Back.

Moving forward, take four steps (RLRL) while hands move upward.
Moving backward, take four steps (RLRL) while hands move down.
Repeat forward and backward steps.

Step 3: Interlude: Clapping.

Facing center, stand in place and clap hands four times.

Step 4-5: Foot Placing.

For a definition of foot placing, see page 225.
With weight on R, touch L toe sideways while extending arms to
sides (1 ct).
Bring toe back beside R while clapping once (1 ct).
Repeat toe touches and arm action three more times.

SULAM YAAKOV

ISRAEL

BACKGROUND

Sulam Yaakov (soo-LAHM yah-KOVE) is one of the newer Israeli folk dances that has become popular internationally. A young nation, Israel has been productive creating many new folk dances. The dances are for young people and carry with them a unique spirit and dash.

MUSIC (4/4)

"Sulam Yaakov" (Jacob's Ladder), 10016, Worldtone (see Folkraft).

FORMATION

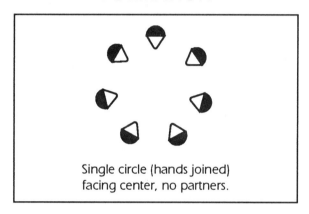

Single circle (hands joined)
facing center, no partners.

COUNTS	STEPS
16	Introduction (wait in place)
32	**1. The Square (Step-Close-Step/Step and Step)** Moving CCW with hands joined, step sideways RLR (step-close-step-hold) 4 cts. Moving toward center, step forward on L (2 cts) and backward on R (2 cts). Moving CW, step sideways LRL (step-close-step-hold) 4 cts. Moving away from center, step backward on R (2 cts) and backward on L (2 cts). Repeat square (16 cts).
32	**2. Grapevine** For a definition of the grapevine, see page 227. Step sideways on R (2 cts) and touch L toe in front of R (2 cts).

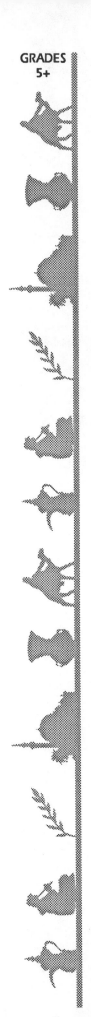

Moving CCW, step L behind R, step sideways on R, step L across R, pivot 1/2 turn on L to face slightly CW (4 cts).

Moving CW, step R across L, step sideways on L, step R behind L, and lift on R extending L, ending almost facing CCW (4 cts).

Moving CCW, step L across R, step sideways on R, step L behind R, and lift on L extending R, to end facing center (4 cts).

Repeat grapevine (16 cts).

64   **3. The Square/Grapevine**
Repeat Steps 1 and 2.

48   **4. The Square (6/8 tempo)**
Moving CCW, step sideways on R (2 cts), close L to R (1 ct), step sideways on R (3 cts).

Moving toward center, step forward on L (3 cts) and forward on R (3 cts).

Moving CW, step sideways on L (2 cts), close R to L (1 ct), step sideways on L (3 cts).

Moving away from center, step backward on R (3 cts) and backward on L (3 cts).

Repeat square (24 cts).

48   **5. Grapevine (6/8 tempo)**
Step sideways on R (3 cts) and touch L toe in front of R (3 cts).

Moving CCW, step on L behind R (2 cts), step sideways on R (1 ct), step on L across R (2 cts), pivot 1/2 turn on L to face slightly CW (1 ct).

Moving CW, step on R across L (2 cts), step sideways on L (1 ct), step on R behind L (2 cts), and lift on R foot extending L (1 ct).

Moving CCW, step on L across R, step sideways on R, step on L behind R, and lift on L extending R (6 cts).

Repeat grapevine (24 cts).

96   **6. The Square/Grapevine**
Repeat Steps 4 and 5 (6/8 tempo).

VARIATIONS AND SUGGESTIONS

Primary

Step 1: Same

Step 2: Step sideways on R (2 cts) and touch L toe in front of R (2 cts).
Moving CCW, step on L behind R, step sideways on R, step on L across R, and bring R beside L ankle (4 cts).

Moving toward center, step forward RLR with a two-step and hold (4 cts). Moving away from center, step backward LRL with a two-step and hold (4 cts). Repeat (16 cts). For a definition of the two-step, see page 226.

ALI PASA

TURKEY

BACKGROUND

The largest minority group in Turkey are the Kurds. They are nomadic herdsmen living as their ancestors did—in caves and temporary shelters—moving as needed to graze their livestock.

·Ali Pasa (AL-ee PASH-a) is one of a number of Turkish dances enjoyed by folk dancers in recent years.

MUSIC (5/4)

BOZ-OK 102, Side 1 Band 1, Bora Ozkok (Ed Kremers' Folk Showplace).

FORMATION

Single line or semicircle (hands
joined at shoulder height in W position).
For a definition of the W position, see page 227.

COUNTS   STEPS

Introduction (wait in place and begin on vocal)

32 **1. Walk Forward-Backward/Walk Center-Back**
Facing R in a line, walk RLR and point L toe
diagonally forward (4 cts).
Still facing R, walk backward LRL and stamp R beside
L (4 cts).
Repeat walks, but move forward (dancers' shoulders
adjacent) RLR and point L toe (4 cts).
Walk backward (shoulders still adjacent) LRL and
stamp R (4 cts).
Repeat Step 1 (16 cts).

32 **2. Grapevine**
For a definition of the grapevine, see page 227.
Facing front (dancers' shoulders adjacent), step
sideways on R, step on L behind R, step sideways
on R, step L in front of R (4 cts).
Again, step sideways on R, step on L behind R, step sideways on R, and close L to R (weight ends on R) 4 cts.

Repeat grapevine to the L (8 cts).
Repeat grapevine to R and L (16 cts).
(Remember, there is a slight pause on each fourth count.)

8   **3. Cross and Step**

Facing front, cross R over L ankle touching R toe beside L and hold (2 cts).
Uncross and step on R (1 ct) and stamp L beside R (1 ct).
Cue the step by saying, "Cross-touch-step-stamp."
Repeat cross-touch-step-stamp (4 cts).

8   **4. Rock**

Facing front, step forward on R, step in place on L, step on R beside L, and extend L toe forward a short step (4 cts).
Step backward on L, step on R beside L, step forward on L, and stamp R beside L (4 cts).

16   **5. Cross and Step/Rock**

Repeat Steps 3 and 4.

VARIATIONS AND SUGGESTIONS

Step 4

Take a short step forward on R, step on L in place, step R beside L, stamp L beside R. Repeat.

NORTH AMERICA

GAMES AND DANCES

United States

Canada

United States

Nova
Scotia

CATCH THE BALL

CANADA

TYPE

Active classroom game

SOMETHING ABOUT THE COUNTRY

Canada is the second largest country in the world and lies between the now disbanded Soviet Union and the United States. The people of Canada come from various backgrounds. Many are of German, Asian, Italian, or Ukrainian descent, but a large percent are either of British or French ancestry. French Canadians, most of whom live in Quebec, speak French.

EQUIPMENT

✔ Nerf ball

FORMATION

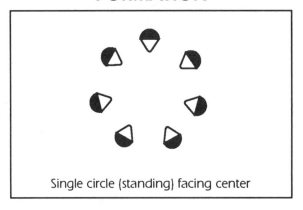

Single circle (standing) facing center

DESCRIPTION

Players toss the ball to each other across the circle keeping the ball in motion as long as possible. If a player fails to catch a toss, he or she is out of the game. If a player tosses the ball in such a manner that it is impossible for another player to catch it, he or she is out. The game is over when there is only one player left in the circle. Make the game more difficult by inviting players to take various positions (sitting, kneeling, or lying on stomach) to catch the ball, or by using different sizes and types of balls.

RATTLER

NATIVE AMERICAN

TYPE
Quiet classroom or playground game

SOMETHING ABOUT THE COUNTRY
The Rattler is a Native American game originating somewhere in the Southwestern section of the United States. The exact tribe the game originated from is not known. There are over 150 different Native American tribes currently living in North America.

EQUIPMENT
✔Blindfolds
✔Tin box (with a pebble inside)

FORMATION

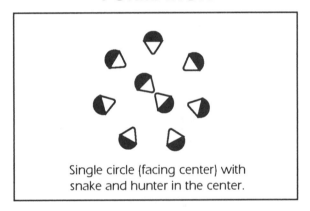

Single circle (facing center) with
snake and hunter in the center.

DESCRIPTION
Blindfold two players in the center of the circle (the snake and the hunter). Give the snake the tin box with the pebble inside. Place the snake and hunter 10-12' apart and choose a leader to give the signal to begin. The snake then rattles the box to give clues to the hunter. The hunter listens carefully and tries to catch the rattler. The snake should move silently and rattle the box two or three times every ten seconds. The leader watches to be sure that neither player collides with the other or with a circle player. The leader can shout "stop" if a potential problem arises and both players must immediately freeze. When the rattler is caught, the hunter becomes the new rattler for the next game and the rattler chooses a new hunter.

SPINNING TOPS
UNITED STATES

TYPE
Active classroom game

SOMETHING ABOUT THE COUNTRY
The Inuit Indians in Alaska have lived in the Arctic region for thousands of years. While they live in modern houses now instead of tents or igloos and purchase store-bought clothing, they maintain their traditional occupations of fishing, hunting, and trapping.

EQUIPMENT
✔Spinning top or disk (such as a Frisbee or coffee can lid)

FORMATION

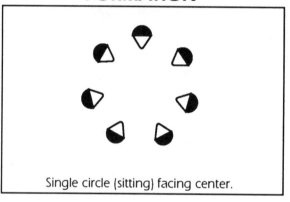

Single circle (sitting) facing center.

DESCRIPTION
Children spin tops in the circle, run out and around the circle and then back in. Choose a player to go to the center of the circle and spin the top or disk. The player then runs around the circle and tries to get back to the center before the top stops spinning.

CIRCLE VIRGINIA REEL

UNITED STATES

BACKGROUND

Square dancing is a lively type of American folk dancing involving groups of four couples. The directions for the dance are given by a caller. Most music for square dancing is provided by fiddles, banjos, and guitars. The Circle Virginia Reel is actually a composite of basic square dance figures. Done in a circle formation, this mixer invites dancers to join in the fun.

MUSIC (2/4)

"Circle Virginia Reel" (with calls), America Dances 57, Educational Activities.

FORMATION

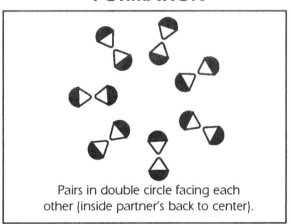

Pairs in double circle facing each other (inside partner's back to center).

COUNTS	STEPS
8	Introduction (wait in place)
16	**1. Forward/Backward** Facing partner, advance three steps (inside partner begins on L, outside partner on R) and then hold out open palms and touch both hands with partner (4 cts). Take three steps backward (4 cts). Repeat forward and back (8 cts).
16	**2. Star R and L** For a definition of the star R and L, see page 226. Facing partner, join R hands (elbows bent, forearms adjacent) and circle CW eight steps back to original place. Facing partner, join L hands and star L, taking eight steps CCW and ending in original place.

8   **3. Two Hands Around**

Facing partner, join both hands (inside partners' palms up, outside partners' palms down) with bent elbows. Circle once CW with eight walking steps.

8   **4. Do-Sa-Do/Veer**

For a definition of the do-sa-do, see page 226.

Taking eight steps, partners pass R shoulders, back to back, L shoulders veering R to meet a new partner.

16   **5. Heel-Toe/Slide**

Joining both hands with new partner, inside partner hops on R while extending L heel to the side (1 ct) and then hops on R again while touching L toe beside R (1 ct).

Same partner repeats heel-toe (2 cts).

Same partner slides sideways L three slides and touches R beside L (4 cts).

Same partner hops on L while extending R heel to the side (1 ct) and then hops on L again while touching R toe beside L (1 ct).

Same partner repeats heel-toe (2 cts).

Same partner slides sideways R three slides and touches L beside R (4 cts).

(At the same time, outside partner does the same heel-toe steps and slides beginning on opposite foot, so facing partners are moving in the same direction.)

16   **6. Swing**

For a definition of the swing, see page 227.

Hooking R elbows, joining R forearms, or joining two hands, partners swing CW in place for 12 cts with a walking step. Take 4 cts to mark time and face CCW in promenade position.

16   **7. Promenade (Walk)**

For a definition of the promenade, see page 226.

Facing CCW, promenade (walk) with partner forward with 16 steps.

Partners end facing each other to repeat dance.

VARIATIONS AND SUGGESTIONS

Step 4

In the beginning, omit the veer and retain the partner. Stop after a couple of repetitions and have inside partners move up a place.

Step 7

Use the traditional cross-hands promenade position or simply join inside hands with partner.

ELVIRA

UNITED STATES

BACKGROUND

Like Amos Moses (see page 185), this dance has become a standard folk dance enjoyed by all recreational dancers. The Elvira is a lively dance with no partners. The dancers face all four walls, very much like the country western dance called "The Four Corners." Texas is thought to be where this dance originated with its square-dance characteristics.

MUSIC (4/4)

"Elvira" or "Texas Twist," Dynamite Dances You Can Do 600, Educational Activities.

FORMATION

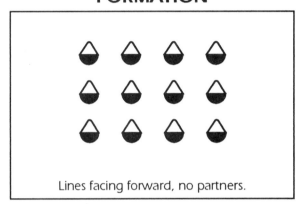

Lines facing forward, no partners.

COUNTS	STEPS

16   Introduction (wait in place)

8   **1. Grapevine R and L**
For a definition of the grapevine, see page 227.
Moving R, step sideways on R, step on L behind R, step sideways on R, and touch L beside R (4 cts).
Moving L, step sideways on L, step on R behind L, step sideways on L, and touch R beside L (4 cts).

4   **2. Walk Backward and Touch**
Moving directly backwards, step RLR and touch L beside R.

4   **3. Two-Step and Turn (Scoot)**
For a definition of the two-step, see page 226.
Step forward on L, close R to L, step forward on L and pivot 1/4 turn L with R toe trailing by L.

VARIATIONS AND SUGGESTIONS

Step 1

Do a simple two-step (step-close step-touch) to the R and L.

Step 3

Rock forward on L, rock backward on R, and rock forward on L while swinging R bent knee forward and making 1/4 turn L. Cue the step by saying, "Rock, two, three, swing."

Formation

The 1/4 turn L in Step 3 causes dancers to face a new wall with each repetition of the dance.

LA BASTRINGUE

FRENCH CANADIAN

BACKGROUND

Quebec is Canada's largest province. Most of the people in Quebec are French Canadians. French is the official language and French culture dominates throughout the province.

La Bastringue (lah bah-STRANG) has been on folk dance programs throughout the country for many years. Its popularity stems from being an essentially easy mixer and is usually danced as part of a long quadrille, a French square dance performed by four couples.

MUSIC (2/4)

"La Bastringue," Dances of Quebec 45 8003 or "One Horse Reel" or "Whirlpool Hoedown," Square Dance Variations 599, Educational Activities.

FORMATION

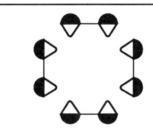

Pairs in single circle with hands joined at shoulder height in W position. For a definition of the W position, see page 227.

COUNTS	STEPS
8	Introduction (wait in place)
16	**1. Forward-Backward** Moving toward center, take three steps forward RLR and touch L beside R (4 cts). Moving away from center, take three steps backward LRL and touch R beside L (4 cts). Repeat Step 1 (8 cts).

16

2. Two-Step CW and CCW

For a definition of the two-step, see page 226.

Moving CW with hands joined, take four two-steps (RLR, LRL, RLR, LRL) 8 cts.

Maneuver on the last two-step to face CCW.

Moving CCW, take four two-steps (RLR, LRL, RLR, LRL) 8 cts.

16

3. Turn-Swing Partner

For a definition of the swing, see page 227.

Partner on R releases R hand, but retains L joined with partner. Same partner turns his or her partner once around under joined hands as other partner takes four walking steps (4 cts).

Swing partner CW with "Buzz" steps (12 cts) pushing off with the L toe on the up-beat and stepping in approximately the same place each time with the R. For a definition of the "Buzz" step, see page 225.

End side by side with inside hands joined facing CCW.

16

4. Promenade with Two-Step

For a definition of the promenade and the two-step, see page 226.

Moving CCW, step forward with eight two-steps beginning R (RLR, LRL, and so on).

On the last two-step, face center and rejoin hands in a single circle.

VARIATIONS AND SUGGESTIONS

Step 3

Omit turning the partner. Partners face and take two hands or hook R elbows and swing with walking steps.

Step 4

In place of two-steps, take 16 walking steps forward CCW.

"Buzz" Step

The feel is as if you are pushing a scooter forward in a line with one foot. The R foot is "glued" to one spot while the L foot is the pusher.

AMOS MOSES

UNITED STATES

BACKGROUND

In every epoch of the American dance scene, there has been a dance that sweeps the nation and is acclaimed by all. Amos Moses (Alligator Stomp,) which has been around for 10 to 15 years, fits this category. This no-partner dance is fun for all.

MUSIC (4/4)

"Alligator Stomp," America Dances 57, Educational Activities, or "Amos Moses," 4-42661, Columbia, or "Amos Moses," 447-0896, RCA Gold Standard (see Ed Kremers' Folk Showplace).

FORMATION

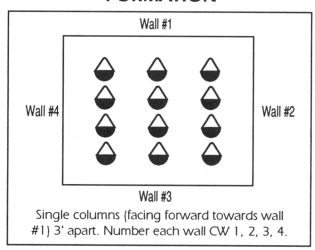

Wall #1

Wall #4

Wall #2

Wall #3

Single columns (facing forward towards wall #1) 3' apart. Number each wall CW 1, 2, 3, 4.

COUNTS   STEPS

16   Introduction (wait in place)

4   **1. Heel Step**
     Facing wall #1, extend R heel slightly forward R, then step on R beside L (2 cts).
     Extend L heel slightly forward L, then step on L beside R (2 cts).

4   **2. Grapevine/Turn**
     For a definition of the grapevine, see page 227.
     Make a 1/4 turn L while stepping sideways on R (R hip pointing toward wall #1 and body facing wall #4) 1 ct. Cross L in back of R (1 ct), step sideways on R (1 ct), and pivot a 1/2 turn R, clapping hands and facing wall #2 (1 ct). Cue the step by saying, "R-back-step-turn."

24

3. Heel Step/Grapevine/Turn

Repeat Steps 1-2 beginning facing wall #2 and
ending facing wall #3 (8 cts).

Repeat Steps 1-2 beginning facing wall #3 and
ending facing wall #4 (8 cts).

Repeat Steps 1-2 beginning facing wall #4 and
ending facing wall #1 (8 cts).

VARIATIONS AND SUGGESTIONS

Step 2

More experienced dancers can add a shoulder dip on the grapevine.

Formation

Note that the dance begins in columns with dancers standing one
behind the other. At the end of the first sequence, dancers are in lines
standing side by side (shoulders adjacent). The steps of this dance are easy.
It is the alignment that gives the trouble.

Place less-experienced dancers in the middle of the columns at the
beginning of the dance and more-able dancers at the front and back of the
columns.

Use a square of paper to help dancers visualize the formation pattern.
Relate each side of the square to the four walls in your classroom.

FLOWERS OF MAY

NOVA SCOTIA

BACKGROUND

In the Scottish tradition, pipers and fiddlers often perform at dances in Nova Scotia. This country's ties to Scotland date back to 1773. Most of the people in Nova Scotia are of British or French ancestry. English, French, and Gaelic are all spoken here.

Flowers of May is an adaptation of a partner dance from Nova Scotia called "The Mayflower."

MUSIC (2/4)

"My Love Is But a Lassie Yet," 1456, Folkraft, or "Gordo's Quadrille," SD-002, Jack Murtha Enterprises.

FORMATION

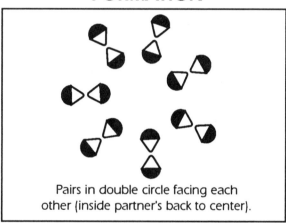

Pairs in double circle facing each
other (inside partner's back to center).

COUNTS	STEPS
16	Introduction (wait in place)
16	**1. Balance R and L/Change Sides** Balance to own R by stepping RLR (2 cts). Balance to L by stepping LRL (2 cts). Taking R hands, exchange places in four steps (RLRL) 4 cts. Repeat from beginning and end in original place, facing partner (8 cts).

8

2. Do-Sa-Do
For a definition of the do-sa-do, see page 226.
Do-sa-do passing R shoulders, back to back, and
passing L shoulders with eight steps. End facing.

8

3. Two-Step Balance
For a definition of the two-step, see page 226.
Partners balance forward towards each other with
a two-step RLR (2 cts), backward LRL (2 cts),
forward RLR (2 cts), and backward LRL (2 cts).
On the last two-step (LRL), both partners maneuver
to end side by side facing CCW, inside hands
joined.

16

4. Promenade
For a definition of the promenade, see page 226.
Moving CCW, take four walks forward RLRL and
two two-steps RLR and LRL (8 cts).
Repeat four walks and two two-steps (8 cts).
Partners end facing each other (inside partner's
back to center).

16

5. Backward and Forward
Move backward four steps RLRL and forward RLRL.
Again move backward RLRL. Then veer R, step-
ping RLRL to meet a new partner.

VARIATIONS AND SUGGESTIONS

Step 3
Partners can hold hands on the two-step balance.
Simplify the balance by stepping forward on R and touching L beside R.
Step backward on L and touch R beside L. Repeat all.

Step 4
Moving CCW, take 16 walking steps.

TENNESSEE SATURDAY NIGHT

UNITED STATES

BACKGROUND

In square dancing, the caller is the most important person because he or she calls out the steps the dancers are to do. A good caller makes rhyming dance directions that create interesting dance patterns.

Young folks and the more mature will beckon to the inviting rhythms of this "country" music.

MUSIC (4/4)

"Tennessee Saturday Night," Streamer and Ribbon Activities 578, Educational Activities.

FORMATION

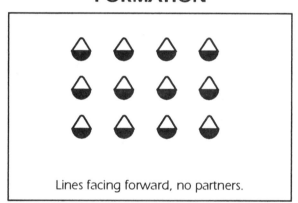

Lines facing forward, no partners.

COUNTS	STEPS
16	Introduction (wait in place)
24	**1. Clap and Hitch** In place, clap hands twice (4 cts) and "hitch" by motioning out-in with R thumb twice (4 cts). Clap twice and hitch with L thumb out-in twice (8 cts). Clap twice and hitch with both thumbs out-in twice (8 cts).
8	**2. Slow Twist** In place, make a slow twist sideways L (2 cts), sideways R (2 cts), sideways L (2 cts), and sideways R (2 cts). Make partial turn on each twist.

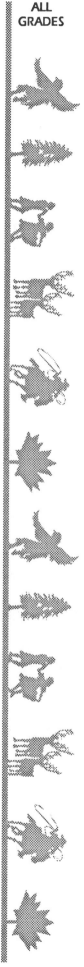

3. Creative Action

Suggestions:

a) Stretch hands up-down, slightly L and R.

b) Shake hands 2 cts by L hip and 2 cts by R hip alternately.

c) Stand in place and hip-rock while swinging hands laterally sideways L and R. For a definition of the hip-rock, see page 227.

d) Extend L heel, then R heel, and then, with feet together, twist twice.

e) Roll bent arms 4 cts and then pull bent elbows backward-forward twice.

f) Extend L foot sideways and back. Extend R foot sideways and back.

g) Do a two-step sideways LRLR. For a definition of the two-step, see page 226.

h) Place arms at sides and slouch L and R with arms moving along legs.

i) Extend L arm sideways-backward and forward-backward. Repeat with R arm.

j) Take two steps followed by two claps.

k) Invite dancers to create their own special steps.

VARIATIONS AND SUGGESTIONS

Step 1

More mature dancers may twist while "hitching." Or, when hitching R, move R toe out-in twice. When hitching L, move L toe out-in twice. When hitching with both thumbs, move both toes out-in twice.

Formation

The dance may also be done in a single circle, facing center.

Creative Movement

Encourage dancers to model their action and teach others.

Invite dancers to practice two or three variations so they can perform them freely.

Movement Exploration Technique

To stimulate creative movement, ask dancers such questions as: What can you do with your hands? What different things can you do with your feet? What can you do with your shoulders? Your knees?

PACObIC

PACIFIC

GAMES AND DANCES

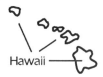

Hawaii

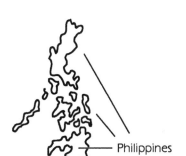

Philippines

New
Guinea

Australia

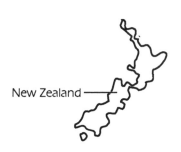

New Zealand

PUSA (CAT AND DOG)

PHILIPPINES

TYPE
Active classroom game

SOMETHING ABOUT THE COUNTRY
In Philippine elementary schools, children are taught in their own dialect for the first two years. After that, the English and Filipino languages are introduced. Children between the ages of 7 and 12 must attend school until at least the sixth grade.

EQUIPMENT
✔Objects (such as shoes, stones, or sticks) to represent bones

FORMATION

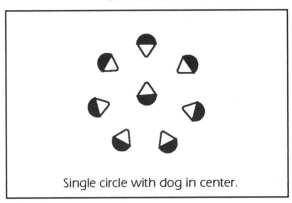

Single circle with dog in center.

DESCRIPTION
Filipino boys and girls are often very quick with their hands and excel at games that require agility, such as this one. Players (cats) form a circle around a pile of shoes, sticks, stones or other objects that represent bones. Choose one player to be the dog. The dog sits near the bones to guard them. The cats try to steal all the bones without getting caught. The dog tries to catch players by tagging them with his or her hands or feet. However, the dog cannot move from where he or she is sitting. If the dog tags a cat, the two exchange places. If the cats get all the bones without getting caught, a new game is started with the same dog.

QUEENIE

NEW ZEALAND

TYPE

Active playground game

SOMETHING ABOUT THE COUNTRY

New Zealand is made up of two major islands. The land on both islands is mountainous with fertile plains. New Zealand is one of the world's leading sheep producers. The country is quite rainy in parts, with as many as 200 inches of yearly rainfall. In addition, there are about 100 earthquakes in New Zealand a year. Because New Zealand lies below the equator, it has summer when the United States has winter.

EQUIPMENT

✔Nerf ball

FORMATION

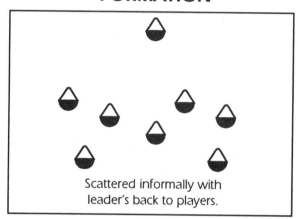

Scattered informally with
leader's back to players.

DESCRIPTION

The leader (Queenie) throws the ball over his or her head. The player who catches the ball before it bounces takes Queenie's place. If the ball bounces, the player who retrieves the ball first holds it behind his or her back. Players put their hands behind their backs and then all players call out "Queenie" and the leader turns around and tries to guess who has the ball. If the leader guesses correctly, he or she gets the ball back and remains the leader. If the leader does not guess correctly, the player who is hiding the ball becomes the new leader.

SHEEP DOG TRIALS

AUSTRALIA

TYPE

Active classroom or playground game

SOMETHING ABOUT THE COUNTRY

While Australia is highly industrialized, like New Zealand, sheep remain very important to the economy. Australia produces about 35% of the world's wool. Australia also boasts some very unique animals, including the koala bear, kangaroo, dingo, emu, and kookaburra.

EQUIPMENT

✔Balloons (two per team)
✔Pieces of cardboard (one per team)
✔Rope

FORMATION

Pens

Balloons OO   OO   OO

Relay lines with two balloons in front of each line.
Sheep pens outlined with rope at opposite
end of lines with openings on the far side.

DESCRIPTION

One player from each team stands at the starting line holding a cardboard flipper ("sheep dog"). The two balloons in front of each team are the "sheep." (Each team should have a different color of balloons.) On the word "go," each player uses the cardboard to flip his or her sheep, one at a time, down the course and into the pen through the entrance. The player who gets two sheep in the pen first scores a point for the team.

The sheep are positioned back at the starting line and the next player on each team has a try. The sheep may only be flipped with the cardboard and not touched in any other way. If a sheep is flipped into the pen other than through the entrance, it must be flipped out again and penned in the proper manner. The team that scores the most points after each member has had a turn is the winner.

VER VER ARAS LAMA

NEW GUINEA

TYPE

Active classroom game

SOMETHING ABOUT THE COUNTRY

New Guinea, the world's second largest island, is covered by tropical rain forests. Many of New Guinea's people supply all their food needs by growing their own food, fishing, hunting, and gathering wild fruits and vegetables. Houses are often built on high platforms for protection.

EQUIPMENT

✔Hula hoops (four)
✔Balls (five, small)

FORMATION

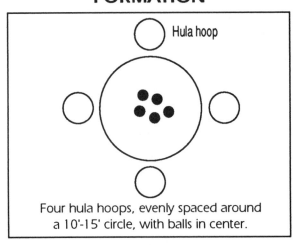

Four hula hoops, evenly spaced around
a 10'-15' circle, with balls in center.

DESCRIPTION

Select a player to stand behind each hula hoop. Players try to collect at least three of the five balls inside their own hoop. Players may take a ball from the center pile or from someone else's hoop. Players may carry only one ball at a time. Players may not prevent other players from taking balls from their own personal hoop. Balls must be placed inside the hoop and not thrown. The first player to have at least three balls inside his or her hoop at one time is the winner.

PA-POHENE

HAWAII

TYPE
Quiet classroom game

SOMETHING ABOUT THE COUNTRY

In the Hawaiian language, each vowel in each word is pronounced completely. For example, the word "noa" is pronounced "noe-ah." Hawaiian words are pronounced as they are written. Try pronouncing the title of this game!

EQUIPMENT
✔Long piece of tapa or other cloth
✔Pebble

FORMATION

Two teams of equal number (6 to 15)
sit in lines facing each other.

One team has possession of the "noa" (pebble). A leader calls out "Puheoheo!" and all the players answer "Puheoheo!" Then three players lift up the cloth to make a curtain between the two teams. One player from the team who has the noa hides the noa with one of his or her teammates. The cloth is removed and all of the players on the team with the noa lean forward and look down, hiding their expressions so they won't give away who has the noa. The other team guesses where the noa is and if they guess correctly, they score one point. If they guess incorrectly, the team with the noa scores a point. The teams take turns hiding the noa. The first team to score ten points is the winner.

APAT APAT

PHILIPPINES

BACKGROUND

The Philippines are composed of over 7,000 islands and islets. At one time, each island had its own form of government. Spanish conquerors brought the islands together under the same rule.

Apat Apat (AH-put AH-put), a delightful dance from the Philippines, is based upon walking steps. The light and inviting music of this mixer makes it popular with all.

MUSIC (2/4)

"Apat Apat," Dances Around the World 572, Educational Activities.

FORMATION

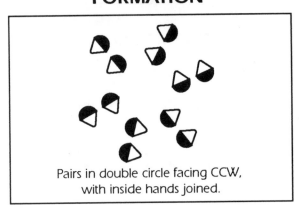

Pairs in double circle facing CCW,
with inside hands joined.

COUNTS	STEPS
8	Introduction (wait in place)
8	**1. Walk Forward-Reverse** Facing CCW, walk forward four steps RLRL. 　Dropping hands, make a 1/2 turn R to face CW 　on the fourth step. Rejoin hands (inside partner's L, outside partner's 　R). Facing CW, walk forward four steps RLRL.
8	**2. Away and Together** Facing partner, back away four steps (RLRL). Facing partner, come together with four steps 　(RLRL).

8   **3. Walk in Opposite Directions**

Partners make a 1/4 turn R, so L shoulders are adjacent.

Facing CW, inside partner takes four steps forward RLRL and four steps backward RLRL.

At the same time, facing CCW, outside partner takes four steps forward RLRL and four steps backward RLRL.

8   **4. Star R and Progress**

For a definition of the star R, see page 226.

Facing partner, join R hands (in a star R with bent elbows and forearms adjacent) and turn CW, RLRL.

Releasing hands, inside partner walks RLRL CCW, and waits to receive a new partner. Outside partner steps RLRL in place ending facing CCW.

VARIATIONS AND SUGGESTIONS

Step 4

Do a star R once around, taking 8 cts instead of a 4 cts and progressing.

Formation

Teaching the dance in a line formation with all pairs facing the same way presents a quicker and easier picture of the action.

Mixer

Before doing the dance as a mixer, do it with a partner. Stop the music and have inside partners advance to the next outside partner.

HUKILAU

HAWAII

BACKGROUND

The Hula is a subtle, graceful, and very traditional Hawaiian folk dance. The special movements of the hands and body by the dancers tell a specific story.

The Hukilau (HOO-key-lau) is one of the happiest, most popular Hawaiian dances and is enjoyed by both children and adults. The words and motions tell the story of a fishing party.

MUSIC (4/4)

"Hukilau," America Dances 57, Educational Activities.

FORMATION

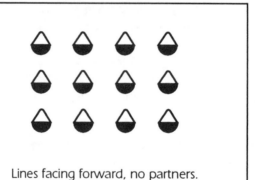

Lines facing forward, no partners.

COUNTS	STEPS
16	Introduction (wait in place)

Part I

8   **1. Oh, We're Going to a Hukilau**

A basic step is continuously repeated throughout the entire dance while hand motions change to pantomime words. The basic step is 4 cts moving R with a step-together-step-tap and 4 cts moving L with a step-together-step-tap.

Moving R with basic step, place L hand on hip and move R thumb out-in twice (4 cts).

Moving L with basic step, pull twice with both hands on R side of body (4 cts).

8   **2. A Huki Huki Huki Huki Hukilau**

Moving R with basic step, pull twice with both hands on L side of body (4 cts).

Moving L with basic step, pull twice with both hands on R side of body (4 cts).

8   **3. Everybody Loves a Hukilau**
Moving R with basic step, extend hands forward and to the sides with palms up (4 cts).
Moving L with basic step, pull twice with both hands on R side of body (4 cts).

8   **4. Where the Lau Lau Is the Kau Kau at the Luau**
Moving R with basic step, "stir and eat" by placing fingers of R hand in palm of L and then bringing fingers up to mouth (4 cts).
Moving L with basic step, move hands out to sides with palms down (4 cts).

8   **5. Oh, We Throw Our Nets Out Into the Sea**
Moving R with basic step, throw both arms forward-backward twice (4 cts).
Moving L with basic step, move alternate hands down-up with palms down to indicate the sea (4 cts).

8   **6. And All the Ama Ama Come Swimming to Me**
Moving R with basic step, place R palm over back of L hand (extending thumbs to side) and move hands up-down (4 cts).
Moving L with basic step, continue moving hands up-down (4 cts).

8   **7. Oh, We're Going to a Hukilau**
Repeat Step 1.

8   **8. A Huki Huki Huki Hukilau**
Repeat Step 2.

Part II

8   **9. What a Beautiful Day for Fishing**
Moving R with basic step, begin with hands by L hip and move hands in an arc above head towards the R (4 cts).
Moving L with basic step, place R bent elbow in L palm and move R hand forward-backward twice as if fishing.

8   **10. The Old Hawaiian Way**
Moving R with basic step, place R bent elbow in L palm and move R hand forward-backward twice (4 cts).
Moving L with basic step, continue moving R hand forward-backward (4 cts).

8 **11. And the Hukilau Nets Are Swishing**
Moving R with basic step, pull both hands twice
on L side of body (4 cts).
Moving L with basic step, move both hands
forward-backward twice (4 cts).

8 **12. Down in Old Laie Bay**
Moving R with basic step and then L, hands
describe a circle (bay) in front of the body with
hands meeting and fingertips touching at the
end.
Repeat Part I, Part II, and Part I again.

8 **13. A Huki Huki Huki, A Huki Huki Huki**
Moving R with basic step, pull both hands twice
on L side of body.
Moving L with basic step, pull both hands twice
on R side of body.

8 **14. A Huki Huki Huki Hukilau**
Point R foot sideways and place hands (palms
ups) out to the sides (2 cts).
Point R foot in front of L and touch hands
together (palms down) 2 cts.
Point R foot sideways and place hands (palms up)
out to the sides (2 cts).
Point R foot forward and extend hands forward
with palms down and R hand on top of L while
inclining head forward (2 cts).

VARIATIONS AND SUGGESTIONS

Vocabulary

hukilau - fishing party
huki - pull
lau lau - beef cooked on a taro leaf, a small bundle of food
kau kau - food
luau - party
ama ama - type of fish

Primary

To simplify, students can sing along while doing the hand motions and
eliminate the steps.

A LA HOY

PHILIPPINES

BACKGROUND

The Philippines have a wide variety of folk dances that reflect a varied cultural mix. A La Hoy is a relatively modern dance and shows Western influences in its style as an easy mixer.

MUSIC (2/4)

"No Te Vayas," 1146, Mico (see Ed Kremers' Folk Showplace).

FORMATION

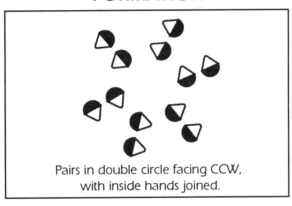

Pairs in double circle facing CCW,
with inside hands joined.

COUNTS	STEPS
8	Introduction (wait in place)
8	**1. Heel-Toe/Two-Step** For a definition of the two-step, see page 226. 　　Extend L heel (1 ct) and then touch L toe beside R (1 ct). 　　Facing CCW, two-step forward by stepping on L, touching R ball of foot beside L, and stepping forward on L (2 cts). 　　Extend R heel (1 ct) and then touch R toe beside L (1 ct). 　　Facing CCW, two-step forward by stepping forward on R, touching L ball of foot beside R, and stepping forward on R (2 cts).

8   **2. Two-Step Balance**

Step slightly to the L on L, touch ball of R beside L, and step on L in place (2 cts).

Step slightly to the R on R, touch ball of L beside R, and step on R in place (2 cts).

Repeat balances to the L and R (4 cts).

8   **3. Heel-Toe/Two-Step**

Repeat Step 1.

8   **4. Two-Step Balance/Progress**

Balance to the L and R as described in Step 2 (4 cts).

Outside partner balances again to the L and R (4 cts) while inside partner progresses forward to a new partner with two-steps LRL hold and RLR hold.

VARIATIONS AND SUGGESTIONS

Step 4

Outside partner may progress forward while inside partner continues two-step balances in place. Also, dancers may progress with four walking steps LRLR rather than the two-steps.

SOUTH AMERICA

GAMES AND DANCES

Columbia

Peru

Brazil

Bolivia

Chile

Paraguay

Argentina

Uruguay

JUEGO DE PAÑUELO (HANDKERCHIEF GAME)

BOLIVIA

TYPE
Active classroom or playground game

SOMETHING ABOUT THE COUNTRY
Colorful piñatas delight children at the many Bolivian festivals. A piñata is a large, hollow papier-mâché container, often in the shape of an animal. It is filled with small toys and treats. One at a time, children are blindfolded and take turns hitting the piñata with a stick. When the piñata breaks, the treasures fall out and the children scramble to pick them up.

EQUIPMENT
✔Handkerchief

FORMATION

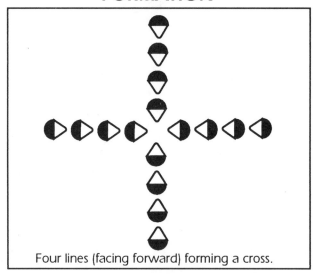

Four lines (facing forward) forming a cross.

DESCRIPTION
A player (IT) circles the group and drops a handkerchief behind a player seated at the end of one of the lines. When the handkerchief is dropped, all players in that particular line must run in a circle around the group and return to their seats in the exact order in which they were originally seated. In the meantime, IT takes one of the vacated seats. The last player to return to position will be without a seat and becomes the new IT.

EL HOMBRE, EL TIGRE, Y EL FUSIL (THE MAN, THE TIGER, AND THE GUN)

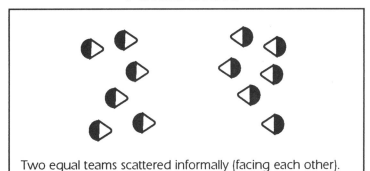

ARGENTINA

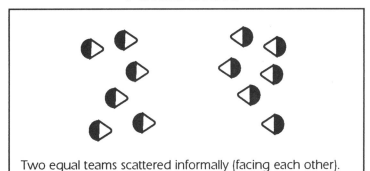

TYPE

Quiet classroom game

SOMETHING ABOUT THE COUNTRY

Many of Argentina's folk dances and folklore are inspired by the spirited Argentine cowboys known as "gauchos." With a lifestyle much like the cowboys of the wild west, gauchos herded wild cattle and horses into the 1800s.

EQUIPMENT

None

FORMATION

Two equal teams scattered informally (facing each other).

DESCRIPTION

Designate a referee to give signals and keep score. The two groups of players go into huddles and secretly decide if they are going to pantomime being a tiger, being a man, or holding a gun. To pantomime the man, players cross their arms over their chest with a confident attitude. To pantomime the tiger, players raise their hands shoulder high and show their claws and teeth. To pantomime holding a gun, players hold one arm out like the barrel of a gun in the attitude of sighting with their R forefinger on the trigger. After huddled players decide on a universal action for their group, both groups turn to face one another. On a given signal from the referee, players from both groups pantomime their chosen action. The winning group is decided by the following standards:

The tiger kills the man, therefore the tiger wins.
The gun shoots the tiger, therefore the gun wins.
The man operates the gun, therefore the man wins.

If both groups choose to pantomime the same action, neither group scores a point. The group that scores ten points first is the winner.

CAT AND RAT

BRAZIL

TYPE
Active classroom game

SOMETHING ABOUT THE COUNTRY
Brazil is the largest country in South America. The Amazon region of Brazil covers almost half of the country and is mainly jungle and tropical rain forest.

EQUIPMENT
None

FORMATION

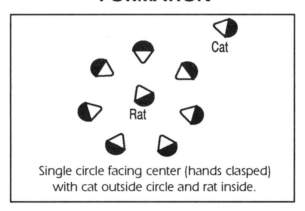

Single circle facing center (hands clasped)
with cat outside circle and rat inside.

DESCRIPTION
Choose one player to be the "cat" and one player to be the "rat." The cat taps one of the players in the circle on the back. The circle player and the cat have the following conversation:

Player: "What do you want?"
Cat: "I want to see the rat."
Player: "You cannot see him or her now."
Cat: "When can I see him or her?"
Player: "At ten o'clock." (The player can say any time he or she desires.)

Immediately, the circle players begin moving CCW in rhythm as they count off the hours by saying, "One o'clock, tick-tock, two o'clock, tick-tock, three o'clock, tick-tock," and so on until they reach the announced time (in this case ten o'clock). At this point, the circle stops moving. The cat steps up again to the player he or she originally tapped.

Player: "What do you want?"
Cat: "I want to see the rat."
Player: "What time is it?"
Cat: "Ten o'clock."
Player: "Alright, come in."

The cat ducks inside under the circle players' clasped hands to try to tag the rat. The rat tries to elude the cat by getting outside the circle. The circle players help the rat by raising their arms and letting him or her pass out of the circle, but hinder the cat by lowering their arms. When the cat catches the rat, the rat selects another cat and the former cat becomes the new rat. If the cat does not catch the rat, the game begins again with the same cat and a new rat.

MANTANTIRULIRULÁ

URUGUAY

TYPE

Quiet classroom game

SOMETHING ABOUT THE COUNTRY

Uruguay is on the Southeastern coast of South America. Most of the country's population lives close to the Southern coast where there are family farms as well as large plantations. The soil is richest on the coastal plains.

EQUIPMENT

None

FORMATION

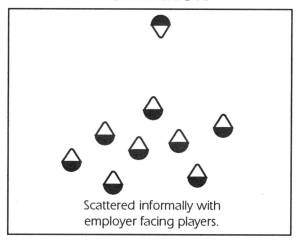

Scattered informally with employer facing players.

DESCRIPTION

Although this game is very popular in Uruguay, it is played everywhere in South America. Mantantirulirulá (man-tan-ti-ruli-rula) is a silly nonsense word without meaning, similar to nonsense words and rhymes made up by English-speaking children. Choose one player to be the "employer." All other players are "workers." The employer and workers recite the following dialogue as all walk freely around the play area:

Employer: "I want someone to work for me. Mantantirulirulá."
Workers: "Which one of us do you want? Mantantirulirulá."
Employer: "I want (names one of the players). Mantantirulirulá."
The named worker: "What work will I do? Mantantirulirulá."
Employer: "You will be a (names some job, such as gardener, cook, secretary, or bookkeeper). Mantantirulirulá."
Other workers: "Do you like the job offered to you? Mantantirulirulá."

The named worker may say "no" and give some silly reason such as "I don't want to be a cook. I'll get too skinny." Other workers chant, "He or she doesn't like that. He or she will get skinny." The employer suggests other jobs until the named worker likes one of them.

At this point, the named worker joins the employer, who chooses another worker and begins suggesting jobs to him or her. The last worker chosen is the employer for the next game.

¿QUIÉN ES? (WHO IS IT?)

CHILE

TYPE

Quiet classroom game

SOMETHING ABOUT THE COUNTRY

Chilean cowboys, called "huasos," are known for their intelligence, wit, and sense of poetry. Huasos enjoy participating in "pallas"—poetry competitions where one huaso starts with one line of original poetry and the rest follow, one by one, supplying the next lines. Sometimes, these competitions last for hours.

EQUIPMENT

None

FORMATION

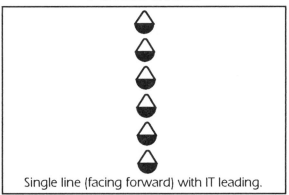

Single line (facing forward) with IT leading.

DESCRIPTION

The leader of the line (IT) begins the game by asking questions. Other players respond in unison.

IT: ¿Has visto a mi amigo? (Have you seen my friend?)
Others: No, Señor or Senorita. (No, Sir or Madam.)
IT: ¿Saben donde esta? (Do you know where he or she is?)
Others: Si, Señor or Senorita. (Yes, Sir or Madam.)

IT takes nine slow steps forward, during which time the other players quickly change their places in the line in any way they wish. One player takes his or her place directly behind IT. Other players begin to call "¿Quién es?" (Who is it?) IT tries to guess which player is directly behind him or her. IT may ask three questions of the other players before he or she guesses:

"¿Es niña o niño?" (Is it a boy or a girl?)
"¿Es alto o bajo?" (Is he or she tall or short?)
"¿Es moreno o rubio?" (Is he or she dark or fair?)

If IT guesses correctly, he or she has another turn. If IT guesses wrong, another player becomes the new IT.

EL ANILLO EN LA CUERDA (THE RING ON A STRING)

COLOMBIA

TYPE
Quiet classroom game

SOMETHING ABOUT THE COUNTRY
The chief export of Columbia is coffee. Coffee plants are usually grown under shade trees and take up to five years to bear fruit.

EQUIPMENT
✔String
✔Small washer

FORMATION

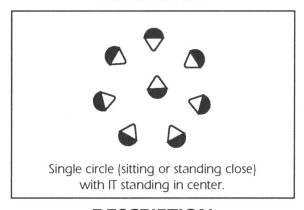

Single circle (sitting or standing close)
with IT standing in center.

DESCRIPTION
Slip the washer (ring) onto the string. Tie the string in a circle so its circumference is the same size as the circle of players. Each player grasps the string in front with both hands, holding it loosely so that the ring can travel easily along the string. Players move their hands along the string by separating their hands (at this point players' hands are touching the hands of their neighbors) and then bringing both hands together in front of them. This movement is continuous throughout the game and by this movement the ring is passed from hand to hand around the circle. As the game starts, the players begin to chant:

The prize is in the hand,
The prize is in the hand,
It passed by here
And left me a flower.

IT tries to guess who has the ring as it is passed along the string. IT catches the hand that he or she supposes is holding the ring and shouts, "Here it is!" If the ring is in the hand that IT selects, the player who holds the ring becomes the new IT. If IT guesses incorrectly, he or she tries again. If IT is unable to locate the ring after several tries, select a new player to be IT.

EL RELOJ
(THE CLOCK)

PERU

TYPE
Active playground game

SOMETHING ABOUT THE COUNTRY
Fishing is an important industry in Peru. In fact, Peru is one of the world's leading fishing countries. Peru works to avoid over-fishing and charges fees to foreign ships for fishing in Peruvian waters.

EQUIPMENT
✔ Jump rope (15-20')

FORMATION

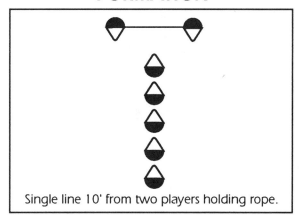

Single line 10' from two players holding rope.

DESCRIPTION
This educational jump rope game, El Reloj (El ray-loh), is loved by all children of Peru. The faster the game is played, the more exciting it becomes for the players. The two rope turners hold the ends of the rope, leaving it slack enough so that as they swing it in a complete circle, it touches the ground. As rope holders turn the jump rope, the first player runs through the rope without a jump. The second player runs in and jumps one time. Players say "one o'clock." The third player follows with two jumps and runs out. Players say "two o'clock." The game continues in this consecutive jump pattern until 12 jumps are executed by a player. If a player touches the rope or misses the correct consecutive number of jumps, he or she exchanges places with a rope turner and the game begins again.

MARAVILLA, MARAVILLA, MBAE MO TEPA—ADIVINA, ADIVINA, ¿QUE SERA? (DEFINE, DEFINE, WHAT IS IT?)

PARAGUAY

TYPE

Quiet classroom game

SOMETHING ABOUT THE COUNTRY

"Nǎn dutí lace," which means "spider web" in the Guarani language of Paraguay, is a unique and famous handcraft. This wonderful tradition is passed from mother to daughter.

EQUIPMENT

None

FORMATION

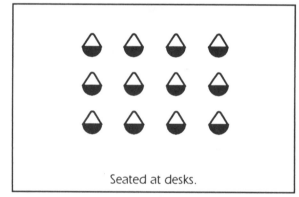

Seated at desks.

DESCRIPTION

This game of definitions is similar to the game of charades. IT describes an object to the group. For example, IT might say, "What has four arms, a woman's head, and moves like this?" Then IT rocks backward and forward, continuing to give clues, such as "It has many colors and six legs." Players may interrupt and make guesses at any time. IT continues to pantomime and give verbal clues. The player who guesses correctly is the next IT. (Answer: A woman sitting in a rocking chair.)

BOSSA NOVA

BRAZIL

BACKGROUND

The Bossa Nova, a Brazilian musical innovation, is an offshoot of the popular Brazilian dance, the Samba. Compared to the Samba, the Bossa Nova has been labeled as "cool jazz." Many versions of this recreational dance have appeared across the United States. Its stimulating and vibrant music is an invitation to all who love to dance.

MUSIC (4/4)

"Bossa Nova," 33079, Columbia (see Ed Kremers' Folk Showplace, or Wagon Wheel Records).

FORMATION

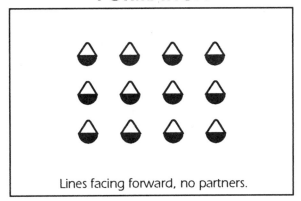

Lines facing forward, no partners.

COUNTS	STEPS
24	Introduction (wait in place)
32	**1. Rock-Rock/Step-Close-Step** Facing front with feet apart, rock in place to the L (2 cts) and to the R (2 cts). Moving sideways L, step LRL hold (4 cts). Cue the step by saying, "Step-close-step-hold." With feet apart, rock to the R and to the L (4 cts). Moving sideways R, step RLR hold (4 cts). Repeat Step 1 (16 cts).

16

2. Squat Jump

Turning slightly L, jump three times on both feet ending
in a squat on the third jump and hold (4 cts).
Turning slightly R, jump three times on both feet ending
in a squat on the third jump and hold (4 cts).
Repeat jump and squat to the L and R (8 cts).
End facing front.

16

3. Sevens

Facing front, step forward on L (1 ct), step backward on R (1 ct), step L beside R (1 ct), step on R
in place (1 ct), step forward on L (1 ct), step
backward on R (1 ct), step on L beside R (1 ct),
and hold.
Beginning on R, repeat seven steps RLRLRLR hold
(8 cts).

VARIATIONS AND SUGGESTIONS

Step 1

Do a basic conga step by stepping sideways on L, stepping on R across
L, stepping sideways on L while turning partially R, and making a low kick
with the R (4 cts). Repeat moving R and kicking L (4 cts). Repeat conga to
L and R (8 cts). Repeat all (16 cts).

Step 3

Simplify by taking seven steps in place.

Mixer

Pairs in a double circle facing each other (inside partner's back to center).
Step 1: Same
Step 2: Same
Step 3: Moving backward, inside partner takes seven short steps LRLRLRL
and holds. Inside partner then veers L to a new partner stepping
RLRLRLR and holds. (Outside partner does the same on opposite feet.)

TANGO

ARGENTINA

BACKGROUND

The world owes Argentina for the Tango, though originally, the dance had African influences as well as influences from Europe and America. In America, the Tango has a different character than the Argentine Tango, but still maintains its cat-like quality. This recreational version of the Tango presents an opportunity to savor its flavor in a no-partner arrangement.

MUSIC (2/4)

"El Choclo," CEM 37023, Twelgrenn Enterprises, or any medium Tango (slow, slow, quick, quick, slow).

FORMATION

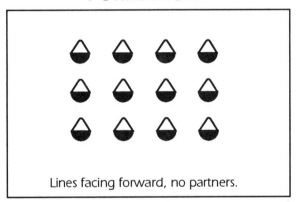

Lines facing forward, no partners.

COUNTS	STEPS
16	Introduction (wait in place)
32	**1. Point and Draw/Walk**

    Facing L, extend and point L toe sideways and hold (2 cts). Draw the L to the R, keeping weight on R (2 cts).

    Facing L, walk forward on L, step on R across L, step sideways on L and pivot to face R while drawing R to L.

    End with weight on L facing R (4 cts).

    Facing R, extend and point R toe sideways and hold (2 cts). Draw the R to the L, keeping weight on L (2 cts).

Facing R, step forward on R, step on L across R, step sideways on R and pivot to face L while drawing L to R.
End with weight on R facing L (4 cts).
Repeat steps facing L and then R (16 cts).

16 **2. Bandit**

Facing front, step sideways on L (2 cts), step forward on R in front of L (2 cts), cross L over R (1 ct), step backward on R (1 ct), draw L beside R (1 ct), and hold (1 ct). Cue the step by saying, "Slow, slow, quick, quick, slow."
Repeat (8 cts).

16 **3. Side Break/Step, Step, Draw**

For a definition of a side break, see page 225.
Facing front, step sideways on L, step on R in place, step on L beside R, and step on R beside L (4 cts).
Repeat side break twice (8 cts).
Step sideways on L, step on R in place, draw L to R and hold (4 cts). Cue the step by saying, "Step, step, draw."

VARIATIONS AND SUGGESTIONS

Step 1

Cue the step by saying, "Point and draw and walk, two, turn."

Step 2

Facing front, extend L heel forward and hold (2 cts).
Touch L toe beside R and hold (2 cts).
Make a 1/2 turn L stepping LRL and hold (4 cts).
Repeat heel-toe on R and 1/2 turn to face front stepping RLR and hold (8 cts).

Formation

Dancers face the front wall, the side wall on the R, and the side wall on the L in the course of this dance.

PROBLEM SOLVING

- **Affirmative**
Ask a question that cannot possibly be answered in the negative.(Solution: "What does y-e-s spell?")

- **Crawl**
Leave the room with two legs and come back with six.(Solution: Return carrying a chair.)

- **Four Feet**
Put four feet against the wall. (Solution: Placing the feet of a chair against the wall.)

- **Hand-to-Hand**
(Give a player some small object to hold in each hand, such as a pencil, eraser, or flower. Ask the player to stretch out both arms full length sideways.) Bring both objects into one hand without bending the elbows so that the hands never come any closer together.(Solution: Place one of the objects on a table. Turn around and pick it up with the other hand.)

- **Haystack**
Make a pile of chairs as high as your head and then take off your shoes and jump over them. (Solution: Jump over the shoes.)

- **Inside and Out**
Kiss a book inside and out without opening it. (Solution: Take the book out of the room and kiss it there. Come back inside the room and kiss the book again.)

- **Safety Point**
Put one hand where the other cannot touch it. (Solution: Placing the R hand on the L elbow, or vice versa.)

- **So Near and Yet So Far**
Stand on an open sheet of newspaper with a friend so that the two of you cannot possibly touch each other. (Solution: Place the newspaper over the threshold of a door and then close the door between the two players.)

STUNTS

- **Cordial Greeting**
(Blindfold two players and place them in opposite corners of the room.) Walk towards each other and shake hands upon meeting.

- **Grasshopper**
Hold one foot up with your hand and hop on the other around the room.

- **Hottentot Tackle**
Cross your arms and grasp your L ear with your R hand and grasp your nose with your L hand. Suddenly release the grasp and reverse the position of the hands (grasp R ear with L hand and nose with R hand). Repeat several times in quick succession.

- **Pilgrimage to Rome**
(The judge announces that the player who is to redeem this forfeit is about to make a pilgrimage to Rome. The judge requests that each member of the company give the player something to take on the journey.) Walk around the room picking up the object each company member is giving you for your journey. When all objects are collected, carry them all once around the room.

- **Lunch Counter**
(Suspend an apple tied to the end of a string from the ceiling, or a pole so it is about head height.) Take a bite from the apple without using your hands.

- **Umbrella Stand**
Rest the tip of a closed umbrella or cane on the floor and hold the top of it with your forefinger. Release the umbrella, spin once around, and grab the umbrella before it falls to the ground.

TASKS

- **Blarney Stone**
Pay a compliment to each person in the room.

- **Little Sunshine**
Walk around the room and give each person a smile.

- **Ennui**
Yawn until you succeed in making someone else yawn.

- **Forum**
Make a speech on any subject assigned by the judge.

- **Jingles**
  (Give a player two pairs of rhyming words.)
  Write a verse of four-line poem using the
  rhyming words.

- **Toast of the Evening**
  Make a toast to your own health by giving a
  complimentary speech about yourself.

- **Verse Lengths**
  Recite a line from a verse, such as "Yankee
  Doodle," counting after each word. For

example, "Yankee (one) Doodle (two) went
(three) to (four) town (five) . . ."

- **Moods**
  Laugh in one corner of the room, sing in the
  second corner, cry in the third, and whistle
  or dance in the fourth corner.

AXIAL MOVEMENTS

Axial movements emanate from the axis of the body while the feet remain stationary. Such movements include bending, swinging, swaying, stretching, pushing, pulling, twisting, curling, shaking, lifting, and collapsing.

LOCOMOTOR MOVEMENTS

Locomotor movements take a person from one place to another. Such movements include:

Walking: Transfer the body weight from one foot to the other.

Running: Transfer weight from one foot to the other faster than a walk. Both feet are momentarily off the floor at the height of a running step.

Leaping: An even transfer of weight from one foot to the other with greater height and spring than a running step.

Jumping: Taking off on one or two feet and landing on both feet.

Hopping: Taking off and landing on the same foot.

Skipping: A step-hop on alternate feet.

Sliding: Smooth leading step and a quicker closing step.

Galloping: A leap with a quicker closing step. The same foot leads in a series of gallops.

BASIC STEP PATTERNS

Bleking

Hop on L extending R heel forward and thrusting R arm forward. Hop onto R extending L heel forward and thrusting L arm forward. Extend feet in rapid succession as RLR while thrusting alternate arms forward. Repeat hopping on R and extending L heel forward (L-R, LRL).

Bleking (page 125)

Bokazo

Hop on L and touch R toe in front of L, hop on L and touch R toe opposite L, jump bringing feet together and hold. May do with opposite feet beginning with hopping on R.

Cshebogar (page 129)
Korobushka (page 143)

Break

Step forward on L, step on R in place, bring L to R and hold. May also do stepping forward on R. For a back break, step backward on L, step on R in place, step on L beside R and hold. May also do stepping backward on R. For a side break, step sideways on L, step on R in place, step on L beside R, and step on R in place. May also do stepping sideways R.

Let's Cha Cha (page 87)
Linda Mujer (page 84)
Tango (page 221)

"Buzz" Step

Do a spot turn CW pushing off with the L foot and stepping in place on the R each time. The feel is as if you are pushing a scooter forward in a line with one foot. The R foot is "glued" to one spot while the L foot is the pusher. May also do CCW pushing off with the R foot.

Atlantic Mixer (page 133)
La Bastringue (page 183)
Limbo Rock Mixer (page 66)

Cross Step

Step on L across R, step sideways on R, step on L across R, and step sideways on R. May also do L stepping on R across L, stepping sideways on L, and so on.

Čerešničky (page 139)
Limbo Rock Mixer (page 66)
Never on Sunday (page 145)

Foot Placing

With weight on R, touch L toe sideways, then bring toe back beside R.

Clapping Dance (page 26)
Mayim Mayim (page 169)

Jarabe

Step forward on L heel, step in place on R ball of foot, bring ball of L beside R. Step forward on R heel, step in place on L ball of foot, bring ball of R beside L.

La Cucaracha (page 82)
La Raspa (page 91)

Running Polka

The polka is a running two-step (step-close-step), 2 cts—RLR, LRL

Kalvelis (page 141)

Running Waltz or Waltz

Moving forward, step LRL and RLR, and so on. The waltz has a "down-up-up" feeling.

Mexican Clap Dance (page 80)
Nixie Dance (page 147)

Schottische

Moving forward, step L-R-L-hop. The free foot may swing forward or be held close to the supporting foot. Also may begin on R. May do forward, sideways, or turning.

Korobushka (page 143)
Savila Se Bela Loza (page 135)

Step-Hop

This is a step and a hop on the same foot.

Bleking (page 125)
Savila Se Bela Loza (page 135)
Tropanka (page 137)

Three-Step Turn

Moving CW in place, make a complete turn, stepping RLR. May also turn CCW, stepping LRL. May also do a four-step turn moving CW and stepping RLR and closing L to R. Or move CCW stepping LRL and closing R to L.

Korobushka (page 143)

Two-Step

Step sideways on L, close R to L, step sideways on L and touch R beside L. Repeat with opposite foot in opposite direction. Cue the step by saying, "Step-close-step-touch."

A La Hoy (page 203)
La Bastringue (page 183)
Clapping Dance (page 26)
Cshebogar (page 129)
Elvira (page 181)
Flowers of May (page 187)
Korobushka (page 143)
Limbo Rock (page 64)
Limbo Rock Mixer (page 66)
Never on Sunday (page 145)
Sulam Yaakov (page 171)
Tennessee Saturday Night (page 189)

Waltz Balance

Step sideways on L, step on ball of R beside L and hold. Step sideways on R, step on ball of L beside R and hold. May also balance forward or backward.

La Cucaracha (page 82)

SQUARE DANCE MOVEMENTS

Do-Sa-Do

Partners pass R shoulders, back to back, and pass L shoulders (making a circle pattern around each other).

Atlantic Mixer (page 133)
Circle Virginia Reel (page 179)
Flowers of May (page 187)

Grand R and L

Partners face and grasp R hands to pull by and extend L hand to next dancer. Pull by with L hand to extend R hand to next dancer. Continue moving around circle extending alternate hands. If outside partners move CW then inside partners move CCW. May end with swing or promenade.

Kalvelis (page 141)

Promenade

Partners stand side by side facing the same direction. Inside partner joins R hand with outside partner's R and L hand with outside partner's L in a traditional crossed position. To simplify, partners may join inside hands. May promenade CCW or CW.

Atlantic Mixer (page 133)
La Bastringue (page 183)
Circle Virginia Reel (page 179)
Flowers of May (page 187)

Star R or L

For a star R, partners join R hands at shoulder level with elbows bent and forearms adjacent and turn once around. For a star L, partners join L hands.

Apat Apat (page 198)
Atlantic Mixer (page 133)
Circle Virginia Reel (page 179)
Linda Mujer (page 84)
Rijpe Gerst (page 151)

Swing

Partners may swing with an elbow hook, arm grasp, or two-hand grip. The traditional square dance swing position is a closed position with R hips adjacent. Dancers can swing with skipping steps, "Buzz" steps, two-steps, or walking steps.

Atlantic Mixer (page 133)
La Bastringue (page 183)
Chimes of Dunkirk (page 119)
Circle Virginia Reel (page 179)
La Raspa (page 91)
Rijpe Gerst (page 151)
Shoes-a-Dancing (page 127)

"POP" DANCING MOVEMENTS

Double Extend

Extend R foot sideways R, touch R beside L, extend R to side again, and step on R beside L. Extend L foot sideways L, touch L beside R, extend L to side again, and step on L beside R. May also do this step either extending L or R backward.

Pata Pata (page 33)

Get Down

Step forward on L with knee bent, step in place on R and straighten, step on L beside R, and step on R in place. May also begin stepping with R forward. May do "over and back" by stepping forward on L, stepping in place on R, stepping on L in back of R, and stepping on R in place.

Around We Go (page 163)
Linda Mujer (page 84)

Grapevine

Moving CW, step on R across L, step sideways on L, step on R behind L, step sideways on L. Or, moving CCW, step on L across R, step sideways on R, step on L behind R, step sideways on R.

Ali Pasa (page 173)
Amos Moses (page 185)
Around We Go (page 163)
Čerešničky (page 139)
Elvira (page 181)
Mayim Mayim (page 169)
Never on Sunday (page 145)
Sulam Yaakov (page 171)
Troika (page 131)

Hip-Rock

Standing with feet astride, rock hips sideways L and R, swinging both arms sideways L and R at the same time.

Clapping Dance (page 26)
Tennessee Saturday Night (page 189)

Single Extend

Extend R foot sideways R and step on R beside L. Extend L foot sideways L and step on L beside R.

Pata Pata (page 33)

W Position

Dancers stand next to each other with elbows bent and hands joined together at shoulder height.

Ali Pasa (page 173)
La Bastringue (page 183)
Never on Sunday (page 145)
Tropanka (page 137)

Ed Kremers' Folk Showplace
155 Turk Street
San Francisco, CA 94102

Educational Activities, Inc.
P.O. Box 87
Baldwin, NY 11510

Festival Records
2773 West Pico Blvd.
Los Angeles, CA 90006

Folkraft/Dance Record Distributors
P.O. Box 404
Florham Park, NJ 07932

Jack Murtha Enterprises
146 Clinton Street
Yuba City, CA 95991

Twelgrenn Enterprises, Inc.
P.O. Box 216
Bath, Ohio 44210

Wagon Wheel Records/Bob Ruff
8459 Edmaru Ave.
Whittier, CA 90605

Windsor Records
5330 N. Rosemead Blvd.
Temple City, CA 91780

GAMES BIBLIOGRAPHY

Anderson, Carolyn J. "A Collection of Hmong Games." Master's thesis, University of Wisconsin-Milwaukee, School of Curriculum and Instruction, 1986.

Arnold, A. "The Work Book of Children's Games." New York: World Publishing, 1972.

Avedon, E. and B. Sutton-Smith. "The Study of Games." New York: John Wiley and Sons, 1971.

Baldwin, G. "Games of the American Indian." New York: Grosset & Dunlop, 1969.

Ball, W. W. "Fun with String Figures." New York: Dover Publications, 1971.

Bell, R. C. "Board and Table Games from Many Civilizations." New York: Dover Publications, 1979.

Bernarde, Anita. "Games from Many Lands." New York: Sayre Publishing, 1970.

Bette, Henry. "The Games of Children: Their Origin and History." Detroit: Singing Tree Press, 1968.

Brandreth, Gyles. "The World's Best Indoor Games." New York: Pantheon, 1982.

Caballero, J. and D. Wilordy. "Children Around the World." Atlanta: Humantics Limited, 1984.

Cassidy, J. and D. Waller. "The Hacky-Sack Book." Palo Alto, California: Klutz Press, 1982.

Castenada, D. "Personal Compilation of Games from the Philippines." Manila, 1981.

_____. "Games of the North American Indians." New York: Dover Publications, 1975.

Dauer, V. and R. Pangrazi. "Dynamic Physical Education for Elementary School Children." Minneapolis: Burgess Publishing, 1986.

Disney, Dick. "Materials Developed from American Indian Culture-Based Curriculum Workshop." 24-28 October in Tacoma, Washington, 1978.

Dunn, Opal. "Let's Play Asian Children's Games." Toyko: Asian Cultural Centre for UNESCO, 1978.

Durojaiya, Susan M. "Children's Traditional Games and Rhymes in Three Cultures." Educational Research (June 1977): 223-26.

Ebbeck, Frederick H. "Learning from Play in Other Cultures." Childhood Education 48 (November 1971): 69-74.

Fait, H. F. "Physical Education For the Elementary School Child." Philadelphia: W. B. Saunders, 1976.

Falkner, E. "Games Ancient and Oriental and How to Play Them." New York: Dover Publications, 1961.

Ferretti, F. "The Great American Book of Sidewalk, Stoop, Dirt, Curb and Alley Games." New York: Workman Publishing, 1975.

Fluegelman, A. "The New Games Book." Garden City, NY: Doubleday, 1976.

_____. "More New Games." Garden City, NY: Doubleday, 1981.

Freeman, Larry. "Yesterday's Games." New York: Century House, 1970.

Gomme, Alice Bertha. "The Traditional Games of England, Scotland, and Ireland." New York: Dover Publications, 1964.

Graham, G.; Holt-Hale, S.; McEwen, T.; and M. Parker. "Children Moving: A Reactive Approach to Teaching Physical Education." Palo Alto, California: Mayfair Publishing, 1980.

Grumberg, M. I. "Some Games of Asia." Singapore: Singapore Press, 1974.

Grunfeld, M. I. "Some Games of the World." New York: Holt, Rinehart and Winston, 1975.

Gryski, C. "Cat's Cradle, Owl's Eyes: A Book of String Games." New York: William Morrow and Co., 1984.

Gurnoe, Katherine J. "Indian Games." Minneapolis, Minnesota: Minneapolis Public Schools, 1971.

Hunt, Sarah. "Games and Sports the World Around." New York: Ronald Press, 1964.

International Council on Health, Physical Education and Recreation, "ICHPER Book of Worldwide Games and Dances." Washington, D. C.: ICHPER, 1967.

Ickis, Margurite. "Book of Games and Entertainment the World Over." New York: Dodd, Mead & Co., 1968.

Jernigan, S. and C. L. Vendien. "Playtime: A World Recreation Handbook." New York: McGraw-Hill, 1972.

Lopez, Mellie Leandicho. "A Study of Philippine Games." Quezon City: University of Philippines Press, 1980.

Los Angeles Unified School District and the Office of Los Angeles County Superintendent of Schools. "Multicultural Games for Elementary School Children." Los Angeles, 1983.

Luke, Moira D. "Multiculturalism and Physical Education." Canada: Non-Classroom Material, 1983.

Macfarlan, A. and P. Macfarlan. "Handbook of American Indian Games." New York: Dover Publications, 1985.

McWhirter, Mary Esther. "The Days That Makes U Happy: Games Around the World." Childhood Education 47 (May 1971): 418-423.

_____. "Games Enjoyed by Children Around the World." Philadelphia: American Friends Service Committee, 1970.

Milberg, A. "Street Games." New York: McGraw-Hill, 1976.

Miller, A. and U. Whitcomb. "Physical Education in The Elementary School." Englewood Cliffs, New Jersey: Prentice-Hall, 1974.

Mitchell, Donald D. K. "Hawaiian Games for Today." Honolulu, Hawaii: Kamehameha Schools, 1975.

Nickell, Pat and Mike Kennedy. "Global Perspectives Through Children's Games." Social Education 51 (March 1987): 2-8.

Opie, I. and P. Opie. "Children's Games in Street and Playground." New York: Oxford University Press, 1984.

Orlick, T. "The Cooperative Sports and Games Book: Challenge with Competition." New York: Pantheon, 1978.

_____. "The Second Cooperative Sports and Games Book." New York: Pantheon, 1982.

Prieto, M. "Play It in Spanish." New York: John Day, 1973.

Roy, Beth. "Play Spans the Ages." Childhood Education 50 (November 1973): 83-89.

Russell, Anna Rita. "Game for Anything: Multicultural Games and Activities for Children." Alberta, Canada: University of Alberta, 1981.

San Diego Unified School District. "Multicultural Games Playing." San Diego, 1987.

Sandoval, Ruben. "Games Games Games = Juegus Juegus Juegus: Chicano Children at Play." Garden City, New Jersey: Doubleday, 1977.

State University of New York, Buffalo, College of Arts and Science. "Games from Around the World." Instructor 79 (October 1969): 56-57.

Strobell, A. P. "Like It Was." "Bicentennial Games 'n Fun." Washington, D. C.: Asbopolis Books Ltd., 1975.

Sutherland, Efua. "Playtime in Africa." New York: Athenuem, 1962.

Sutton-Smith, Brian. "The Folk Games of Children." Austin, Texas: University of Texas Press, 1972.

Torbert, Marianne and Lynne B. Schnieder. "Positive Multicultural Interaction Using Low Organized Games." Journal of Physical Education, Recreation & Dance 57 (September 1986): 40-44.

van Ourenhoven, Nico J. A. "Common Afghan Street Games." Lisse: Swets and Zeitlengete, 1979.

Vinton, Iris. "The Folkways Omnibus of Children's Games." Harrisburg, Pennsylvania: Stackpole Books, 1970.

Weigle, L. M. "Jacks and Jack Games." New York: Dover Publications, 1970.

Whitney, Alex. "Sports and Games the Indians Gave Us." New York: McKay, 1977.

World Association of Girl Guides and Girl Scouts. "World Games and Recipes." London, 1974.

DANCE BIBLIOGRAPHY

Bley, Edgar S. "The Best Singing Games." Sterling, NY: Sterling Publishers, 1963.

Boorman, Joyce. "Creative Dance in Grades Four to Six." Ontario, Canada: Longman Canada, Ltd., 1971.

Braley, William; Kinicki, Geraldine; and Catherine Leedy. "Daily Sensorimotor Training Activities." Baldwin, NY: Educational Activities, 1968.

Casey, Betty. "International Folk Dancing U.S.A." Garden City, NY: Doubleday and Co., 1981.

Cherry, Clare. "Creative Movement for the Developing Child." Carthage, IL: Fearon Teacher Aids, 1962.

Gilbert, Cecile. "International Folk Dance at a Glance." Minneapolis: Burgess, 1974.

Glass, Henry "Buzz." "Vol. 1, Action Time with Story, Chant and Rhyme." Hayward, CA: Alameda County School District, 1973.

_____. Vol. 2, "Action Time with Story, Rhyme and Chant." Hayward, CA: Alameda County School District, 1973.

Hall, J. Tillman; Sweeny, Nancy Hall; and Jody Hall Esser. "Until the Whistle Blows." Santa Monica, CA: Goodyear Publications, 1977.

Harris, Jane A.; Pittman, Anne M.; and Marlys S. Waller. "Dance a While." New York: Macmillan, 1988.

Heaton, Alma. "Fun Dance Rhythms." Provo, UT: Brigham Young University Press, 1976.

Jones, Bessie and Bess Lomax Hawes. "Step It Down." New York: Harper & Row, 1972.

Joyce, Mary. "First Steps in Teaching Creative Dance." Palo Alto, CA: National Press, 1973.

Kraus, Richard. "Folk Dancing: A Guide For Schools, Colleges and Recreational Groups." New York: Macmillan, 1962.

Nelson, Wayne E. and Henry "Buzz" Glass. "The Rainy Day Survival Book." Turlock, CA: Raemax Publications, 1985.

Sannella, Ted. "Balance and Swing." New York: Country Dance Society, Inc., 1982.

Schurr, E. "Movement Experiences for Children." Englewood Cliffs, NJ: Prentice Hall, 1980.

Wakefield, Eleanor E. "Folk Dancing in America." New York: J. Lowell Pratt Co., 1966.

Weikart, Phyllis S. "Teaching Movement and Dance." Ypsilanti, Michigan: High Scope Press, 1982.

INDEX OF GAMES AND DANCES BY COUNTRY

The (g) or (d) following each entry signifies whether the activity is a game or a dance.

Africa

Benin
Cho-Cho-Chuckie (g)

Congo
Ta Mbelle (g)

Egypt
Tug of War (g)

Ghana
Clapping Dance (d)
Kye Kye Kule (d)
Oware (g)

Kenya
Animal Keepers (g)

Liberia
Hop-Sing Game (g)

Nigeria
Mowrah Cawkah (d)
Trapping Tigers (g)

Sierra Leone
Haba Gaba (g)

South Africa
Pata Pata (d)

Sudan
Don-Don Ba Ji (g)

Tanzania
Chikincha (g)

Uganda
Bottle Relay (g)

Asia

Burma
Myan, Myan (I Pass the Shoe from Me to You) (g)

Cambodia
Ang-Konnh (g)

China
Chinese Friendship Dance (d)
Zhao Lingxiu (Find the Leader) (g)

Hong Kong
Chung Tou Teh Tou (Plant Beans, Reap Beans) (g)

India
Kabbaddi (g)

Indonesia
Wora-Wora Tjintjin (Ring and Loose String Game) (g)

Japan
Furoshiki Mawaski (Scarf Passing Game) (g)
Tanko Bushi (d)

Korea
Putung Putung (g)

Laos
Chopsticks Jack (g)

Malaysia
Memutar Pinggan (Plate Spinning) (g)

Pakistan
Sathi Khoj (Lost a Couple) (g)

Sri Lanka
Stations (g)

Taiwan
Clapstick Blind Man's Bluff (g)

Thailand
O-O-Oh- Soom (g)

Vietnam
Kick-Swing (g)

Caribbean

Cuba
Cuba and Spain (g)

Dominican Republic
Thumper (g)

Haiti
Ainsi Font, Font, Font des Zami de Papa La Chaise (Thus Do, Do, Do the Friends of Papa La Chaise) (g)

Jamaica
Sally Water (g)

Puerto Rico
The Stones (g)

Trinidad
Counting Out Game (g)

West Indies
Limbo Rock (d)
Limbo Rock Mixer (d)
Manee Gogo (d)

CENTRAL AMERICA

El Salvador
El Gavilán, la Coneja, y los Conejos (The Hawk and the Rabbits) (g)

Guatemala
Andares–Andares (g)
Pin (g)

Mexico
La Cucaracha (d)
Let's Cha Cha (d)
Linda Mujer (d)
Mexican Clap Dance (d)
El Mosquito (d)
El Periquito (The Little Parrot) (g)
La Raspa (d)
Rima de Gallos (The Cock Fight) (g)

EUROPE

Belgium
Baton Maudit (The Cursed Stick) (g)
Chimes of Dunkirk (d)
Shoes-a-Dancing (d)

Bulgaria
Tropanka (d)

Czechoslovakia
Čerešničky (d)
Zpoved (Confessions) (g)

Denmark
Nixie Dance (d)
Shoemaker's Dance (d)
The Whales (g)

England
Pop Goes the Weasel (d)
Snail Whorl (g)

Finland
Sarvisilla (g)

France
La Bastringue (d)
Chimes of Dunkirk (d)
Swap Chairs by the Numbers (g)

Germany
Atlantic Mixer (d)
Eins Zwei Drei (d)
Unwrap the Chocolate (g)

Greece
Never on Sunday (d)
Syllables (g)

Holland
Alle Vogels Vliegen (All the Birds Fly) (g)
Rijpe Gerst (d)

Hungary
Cshebogar (d)

Iceland
In-and-Out-the Windows (g)

Ireland
Little Irish Dance (d)
Pass the Orange (g)

Italy
Il Cucuzzaro (The Pumpkin Planter) (g)

Lithuania
Kalvelis (d)

Poland
Jak Sie Masz (g)

Russia
Korobushka (d)
Troika (d)
Zeros (g)

Scotland
Wee Bologna Man (g)

Spain
Tag (g)

Sweden
Bleking (d)
The Child Is Down (d)
North Winds and the South Wind (g)

Switzerland
Drei-Mann Hoch (Three-Man Deep) (g)

Yugoslavia
Savila Se Bela Loza (d)
Zmirke (g)

MIDDLE EAST

Armenia
Halay (d)

Iran
Goosh Va Damagh (Ear and Nose) (g)

Iraq
Magura (Pecan Hole) (g)

Israel
Around We Go (d)
Bli Yadayim (Without Hands) (g)
Mayim Mayim (d)
Sulam Yaakov (d)
Tzadik Katamar Yifrach (d)

Lebanon
Pebble Toss (g)

Turkey
Ali Pasa (d)
Kukla (g)

NORTH AMERICA

Canada
La Bastringue (d)
Catch the Ball (g)

Native American
Rabbit and the Fox (d)
Rattler (g)

Nova Scotia
Flowers of May (d)

United States
Amos Moses (d)
Circle Virginia Reel (d)
Elvira (d)
Spinning Tops (g)
Tennessee Saturday Night (d)

PACIFIC

Australia
Sheep Dog Trials (g)

Hawaii
Hukilau (d)
Po-Pohene (g)

New Guinea
Ver Ver Aras Lama (g)

New Zealand
Queenie (g)

Philippines
A La Hoy (d)
Apat Apat (d)
Pusa (Cat and Dog) (g)

SOUTH AMERICA

Argentina
El Hombre, el Tigre, y el Fusil (The Man, the
    Tiger, and the Gun) (g)
Tango (d)

Bolivia
Juego de Pañuelo (Handkerchief Game) (g)

Brazil
Bossa Nova (d)
Cat and Rat (g)

Chile
¿Quién Es? (Who Is It?) (g)

Colombia
El Anillo en la Cuerda (The Ring on a
    String) (g)

Paraguay
Maravilla, Maravilla, Mbae Mo Tepa—Adivina,
    Adivina ¿Que Sera? (Define, Define, What
    Is it?) (g)

Peru
El Reloj (The Clock) (g)

Uruguay
Mantantirulirulá (g)

Cho-Cho-Chuckie adapted with permission from Iris Vinton's "The Folkways Omnibus of Children's Games" by Stackpole Books.

Trapping Tigers reprinted with permission of the publishers from "Multicultural Games for Elementary School Children." Copyright © 1983, 1988 Los Angeles Unified School District and Los Angeles County Office of Education.

Bottle Relay adapted with permission from S. Jernigan and C. Vendien's "Playtime: A World Recreation Handbook," copyright © 1972, by McGraw-Hill.

Animal Keepers adapted with permission from Iris Vinton's "The Folkways Omnibus of Children's Games" by Stackpole Books.

Ta Mbelle adapted with permission from Nina Millen's "Children's Games from Many Lands" by Friendship Press.

Haba Gaba adapted with permission from Iris Vinton's "The Folkways Omnibus of Children's Games" by Stackpole Books.

Clapstick Blind Man's Bluff adapted with permission from Iris Vinton's "The Folkways Omnibus of Children's Games" by Stackpole Books.

O-O-Oh-Soom adapted with permission from Constance M. Hallock's "Fun and Festival from Southeast Asia" by Friendship Press.

Stations adapted and reprinted with permission of the American Alliance for Health, Physical Education, Recreation and Dance from the book "ICHPER Book of Worldwide Games and Dances," copyright © 1967.

Memutar Pinggan (Plate Spinning) from "The Second Cooperative Sports and Games Book" by Terry Orlick. Copyright © 1982 by Terry Orlick. Reprinted by permission of Pantheon Books, a division of Random House, Inc.

Putung Putung adapted with permission from S. Jernigan and C. Vendien's "Playtime: A World Recreation Handbook," copyright © 1972, by McGraw-Hill.

Furoshiki Mawaski (Scarf Passing Game) adapted with permission from S. Jernigan and C. Vendien's "Playtime: A World Recreation Handbook," copyright © 1972, by McGraw-Hill.

Kick-Swing adapted with permission from Constance M. Hallock's "Fun and Festival from Southeast Asia" by Friendship Press.

Counting Out Game adapted with permission from Nina Millen's "Children's Games from Many Lands" by Friendship Press.

Ainsi Font, Font, Font des Zami de Papa La Chaise (Thus Do, Do, Do the Friends of Papa La Chaise) adapted with permission from Iris Vinton's "The Folkways Omnibus of Children's Games" by Stackpole Books.

Cuba and Spain reprinted with permission of the publishers from "Multicultural Games for Elementary School Children." Copyright © 1983, 1988 Los Angeles Unified School District and Los Angeles County Office of Education.

Thumper adapted with permission from S. Jernigan and C. Vendien's "Playtime: A World Recreation Handbook," copyright © 1972, by McGraw-Hill.

Rima de Gallos (The Cock Fight) reprinted with permission of the publisher from "Multicultural Games for Elementary School Children." Copyright © 1983, 1988 Los Angeles Unified School District and Los Angeles County Office of Education.

Andares-Andares adapted with permission from "World Games and Recipes" by the World Association of Girl Guides and Girl Scouts.

The following dances are adapted and reprinted with permission from Educational Activities, Inc.:

Kye Kye Kule

Mowrah Cawkah

Pata Pata

Chinese Friendship Dance

Manee Gogo

Mexican Clap Dance

Linda Mujer

Let's Cha Cha

La Raspa

The Child Is Down

Little Irish Dance

Pop Goes the Weasel

Shoes-a-Dancing

Savila Se Bela Loza

Tropanka

Korobushka

Never on Sunday

Nixie Dance

Shoemaker's Dance

Around We Go

Circle Virginia Reel

Elvira

Amos Moses

Tennessee Saturday Night

Apat Apat

Hukilau